DONDA'S RULES

THE SCHOLARLY WORKS OF DR. DONDA WEST (MOTHER OF KANYE WEST)

Edited by
GARRARD McCLENDON, Ph.D.

Wayman Dean Press

Donda's Rules. Copyright © 2020

Editing, compilation, commentary, research, and explanatory notes copyright © 2020 by Garrard McClendon, Ph.D. All rights reserved.

Executor Copyright (C) Kanye West for the Estate of Donda Clairann Williams West.

Printed in the United States of America. No part of this book may be reproduced or copied in physical or electronic form without permission from the publisher.

Wayman Dean Press / Duthga Press and Duthga Academic Press LLC

PO Box 81052

Chicago, IL 60681

FIRST EDITION

Cover design by *Phenix7* Mktg, Inc. Gina Altieri/Betsy Serdar

Cover photo by Taghi Naderzad/Contour by Getty Images

Interior design by Vellum

ISBN-13: 978-0-9968832-0-7

ISBN 978-0-9968832-0-7

Library of Congress Control Number: 2017934359

McClendon, Garrard O., 1966 -

1.English Language. 2.Rhetoric. 3.English Language Style. 4.Black History. 5.African Americans. 6.Linguistics. 7. Test Scores. 8.Black Speech Patterns 9.Ebonics. 10.Systems Theory. 11.Black English. 12.Racism. 13.Education. 14.Schools. 15. Russian Literature. 16.Curriculum 17. Systems Theory. 18.Composition 19.Writing

Printed in the United States of America

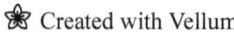 Created with Vellum

DEDICATED TO

*Kanye West
and
The Eckles, Hooks, West, and Williams Families*

"This is the story of a champion…"

— Kanye West, Graduation, 2007

CONTENTS

Remarks	ix
Editor's Introduction	xv
Vita of Donda West	1
Acknowledgments	3
➢ The Educational Philosophy of Donda West	5
➢ A Resolution on Ebonics	7
➢ General Systems Theory and Rhetoric : Toward a New World View for Teachers of Written Composition in Secondary Schools and Colleges - Donda's Rules	9
➢ Systems Approaches and Education	25
➢ Research and Theories in the Teaching of Written Composition	43
➢ Systems Philosophy as the Theoretical Base of Teaching Written Composition	77
➢ Implementing a Systems Approach in the Teaching of Written Composition	101
➢ A Community-Based Economic Development Curriculum for Freshmen in Chicago Public Schools	121
➢ Russian Culture and Literature Implementation Plan	135
Bibliography	139
About the Editor	145

REMARKS

Che "Rhymefest" Smith, Dr. Brenda Eatman Aghahowa, and Donnie Nicole Belcher discuss the professionalism of Donda West as a professor, writer, and organizer.

MEETING KANYE'S MOTHER was like meeting royalty. Her home was adorned with African art, sculptures, statues, and hundreds of books. Dr. West was regal and passionate, with a genuine love for family, friends, and her son's companions.

Kanye introduced me as "Rhymefest," and I remember being angry with him. Dr. West was an elegant professor and I didn't want to be presented by my rap name. I didn't want her to think I was a bad influence. Why wouldn't he introduce me as Che Smith? She may not understand what "Rhymefest" means.

Without missing a beat, with a smile warming my spirit and a tone that removed all apprehension, Dr. West said my name perfectly.

"Hello Rhymefest. Are you about to work on music with Kanye?"
"Yes Ma'am."

I bowed my head in respect, or perhaps, insecurity and embarrassment. I just wanted to be accepted into the West family.

I was amazed that Kanye let his mom hear every song, including those with explicit lyrics. I was accustomed to older people not understanding our expression, expecting lectures on our foul mouths and critiques of our beats. Dr. West listened to our songs. She never diminished us and always gave constructive critique. I fell in love with her majesty. She prepared Kanye's friends for greatness in the same way she nurtured her son for his destiny.

She listened to a song I wrote about selling drugs and killing people.

She asked, "Rhymefest, have you done any of those things you spoke of in the song?"

I blasted, "No, but I want to get on the radio and this is what people want to hear."

In her loving tone, she gave a half-smile and said, "Rhymefest, would you be comfortable being successful at music based on lies?"

I had no come back.

She continued, "Your mother had you as a teen; your father wasn't around. You have a little sister. What do you want for her? Your most profound lyrics haven't been written yet."

Again, I had no reply.

She finished by simply saying,

"Rhymefest, don't lie to yourself or lie to others when creating music. SHARE YOUR TRUTH."

The most valuable lessons I ever learned were from Dr. West. Without ever having to enroll at Chicago State to take a class with her, I was given knowledge of self, by a selfless person who happened to be my friend's mother. Kanye was blessed to have her as a mom; while I was blessed to have her as mentor. She taught me how to share my truth, and it has served me well.

Che "Rhymefest" Smith is a Grammy, Golden Globe, Critics Choice, and Academy Award winner. He is a recording artist, actor, and the co-founder/creative director of Art of Culture, Inc.

Dr. Brenda Eatman Aghahowa

EVERY DAY I think of my friend Donda West. I thank her for her warm spirit, sense of humor, and passion for teaching first-generation African-American college students. Her drive and excellence were instrumental in motivating the campus community and her creative son, Kanye.

I am indebted to Donda for hiring me as a lecturer. She later pushed me to apply for a tenure-track position, but she knew that my credentials would not be adequate for tenure. She gently asked, "Would you be willing to go back to earn a second doctorate?"

Who wants to hear that when you have a spouse and three small children? But I agreed, and enrolled in the Ph.D. program at the University of Illinois at Chicago. She gave me moral and practical support, accommodating me with workable schedules. She was vibrant, sharing laughter in the English Department. She was also generous, often paying conference fees for colleagues.

With a constant push from Donda, I published the book, *Grace Under Fire: Barbara Jordan's Rhetoric of Watergate, Patriotism, and Equality*.

Collaborating with Professor Haki Madhubuti, she offered writers' conferences, sponsored by the Gwendolyn Brooks Center of Black Literature and Creative Writing. Thanks to these conferences, the Chicago State campus was exposed to Nikki Giovanni, Maya Angelou, August Wilson, Toni Morrison, Quincy Troupe, Chernoh Sesay, Sr., Amiri Baraka, Geneva Smitherman, Tim and Daphne Reid, and, of course, Gwendolyn Brooks. Donda also hired literary talents like Quraysh Ali Lansana, Sandra Jackson-Opoku, and poet, Dr. Kelly Norman Ellis.

I keep a photo of Donda on my office desk. It reminded me of our "Motown Mommas" talent show performances. The photo gives me the courage to teach without fear.

I had the painful privilege of coordinating the memorial service held for her on our campus Friday, November 16, 2007. I still ache inside for her untimely passing, and the void has yet to be filled. I love and miss my friend, Donda.

Brenda Eatman Aghahowa, is an associate professor of English at Chicago State University, and ordained minister, and an expert on the late Congresswoman Barbara Jordan.

∽

Donnie Nicole Belcher

THERE ARE no coincidences. Donda West loved the arts and as consultant, teacher, and mentor to creatives, parts of my professional path have mirrored Donda West's career.

When the idea of creating a youth arts organization was born in December of 2011, we decided to become familiar with the teaching and educational philosophy of Dr. West. While very familiar with her parenting philosophy, we wanted to know more about the impact she had in her 31 years as an educator and administrator. What we discovered was a progressive professor whose pedagogy was rooted in empowerment, experiential learning, and cultural sensitivity. Dr. West was writing about the value of black vernacular English, years before it became an academic trend. She was training an army of educators who valued not only who students would become, but who they were when they first entered the classroom.

There are no skills more valuable than literacy and creativity. Donda believed that arts education and higher levels of rhetoric, oratory, and literacy should receive massive funding in low-income communities.

We decided that Art of Culture (formerly Donda's House) would be a safe haven for artists' inspiration. We also decided that our first program, "Got Bars," would nurture aspiring hip-hop artists because the art form is relegated to the margins of musical appreciation. As a college professor and the mother of a hip-hop star, Dr. Donda West represented the balance between popular culture and academic tradition, in the same way that Art of Culture seeks to be a bridge high-profile artists and the communities that gave birth to them.

Arts education should be mandatory. Students who participate in the arts are better problem solvers and have a higher propensity for more positive outcomes. Art of Culture is an incubator for creative genius. Many of our students will go on to become Grammy Award winning writers and artists like Rhymefest and Kanye; some of them may become gallery owners and leaders in the entertainment field. We know that all of them will be goal-oriented, civically engaged problem solvers. With Donda's blueprint, we are creating artists who practice art as an approach to life, going beyond the canvas, the recording, and the stage. The spirit of Dr. Donda West is alive in academia and in the arts, because we always need truth tellers who will advance the culture with creativity.

Donnie Nicole Belcher is a writer, educator, creative and strategic planner, and the Executive Director of Art of Culture, Inc. She is the recipient of the Deloris Jordan Award for Excellence in Community Leadership, an Ebony Power 100 Honoree, and winner of the Echoing Green Fellowship.

EDITOR'S INTRODUCTION

Discovering the Essential Works of a Scholar

Great thinkers captivate you with their ability to create meaningful discourse. They are magnetic, and moments with them are priceless. Donda West was special and truly priceless.

She acknowledged the importance of an individual's purpose. Although her path was academic, she chose not to belittle those who were equally talented and gifted in other disciplines. To paraphrase Kipling, she walked with kings without losing the common touch.

Dr. West's legacy runs deep at Chicago State University. Her stellar teaching career and influence are evident in faculty students who continue to talk about her prowess as an educator, writer, and curriculum developer. Donda was much more than a scholar and social critic. She was a builder of villages.

She was a Fulbright scholar, professor, co-chair of the National Council of Teachers of English, 1998 Outstanding Educator of the Year, chair of the NCTE Black Caucus, member of Who's Who Among Black Americans, consultant, education expert to China, world traveler, and mother to Kanye. Dr. West's scholarly legacy needed to be in print and we found the gems. Few know of her master's thesis and literature reviews on the use of Ebonics. Fewer are aware of her studies on systems theory and rhetoric. Her written works from Chicago Public Schools, Chicago State University, Atlanta University, and Auburn University, show her prolific practice as a writer.

This book includes her philosophy of education, her resolution on Ebonics, systems theory and rhetoric dissertation, her community-based economic development plan, and her Russian Culture and Literature Implementation Plan.

Chicago State University allowed me to create two Donda West curriculum modules for the ED 1520 Foundations of Education class. In these classes, we searched for the essential works of West. After discovering Dr. West's papers, it was much easier for students to craft their own educational philosophy statements.

I am honored to present Donda's Rules and the scholarly documents of Donda West.

Garrard McClendon, Ph.D. is an associate professor of education at Chicago State University. He is the author of Ax or Ask? The African American Guide to Better English, an Emmy Award winner, Associated Press Award winner, and an NAACP Champion Award winner.

VITA OF DONDA WEST

THIS IS THE VITA POSTED IN DR. WEST'S PUBLISHED DISSERTATION.

DONDA CLAIRANN WILLIAMS WEST, daughter of Portwood and Lucille (Eckles) Williams, was born July 12, 1949, in Oklahoma City, Oklahoma. She attended Oklahoma County Public Schools and graduated from Frederick Douglass High School, Oklahoma City, in 1967. In September, 1967, she entered Virginia Union University in Richmond, Virginia, and graduated with honors receiving the degree of Bachelor of Arts (English) in May of 1971. In September of 1971, she entered graduate school at Atlanta University. She received the degree of Master of Arts (English) in August of 1973. Before entering graduate school in September of 1974 at Auburn University, she worked as an English and drama instructor at Morris Brown College in Atlanta, Georgia. She completed doctoral studies from Auburn University in 1980. She married Raymond West (son of James and Fannie (Hooks) West) in January of 1973. They have one son, Kanye Omari West.

ACKNOWLEDGMENTS

For their assistance and support, I thank the CSU Archives, and the English and Education departments at Chicago State University.

For their institutional reputation and cooperation, I appreciate the faculty at Auburn University, Clark Atlanta University, the AUCC, Morris Brown College, and Virginia Union University.

For unconditional love, thanks to Duane and Theodore, Tristin, Jocelyn, Olympia, ReAnne, Jaiman, Maximilian, and Miranda. Thanks to my faith leaders - Elder Eugene and Barbara Rhenwrick.

I offer much gratitude to poet Parneshia Jones and research assistants, Rosa Brito-Valdes, Carla Everett, Mikila Griggs, Monica Jackson, Douglas Jenkins, Delilah Powell, Kenneth Richards, Candis Ridley, Stanley Williams, and special assistant, Collage Warner.

Thanks to board members Exavier Pope, Olivia Gil-Guevara, Todd Walton, and Kelsey Riley.

For confidence and esteem, I thank my wife, Quanica.

1
THE EDUCATIONAL PHILOSOPHY OF DONDA WEST

TEACHERS SHOULD FUSE fine arts instruction, cultural literacy, and experiential learning in order to cultivate the interests of children. To create an intellectually open environment, teachers should be flexible, competent, and student-centered, using "real world" activities. There should be curriculum integration among English, math, science, art and social studies courses. Before a child's promotion to the next grade, higher level skills should be mastered.

A student's home, neighborhood, and historical culture must be embedded into the curriculum. School is relevant when culture, the art, and strong pedagogy are reinforced. Teachers, too often, take the position of dominance rather than the perspective of mind sharing. As Aquinas stated, "it is better to illuminate than merely to shine, to deliver contemplative truths than merely to contemplate." Education creates a sense of meaning and wholeness for students.

Froebel and Dewey's observations of children showed that the practice of playing leads to invention and cognitive development. Children learn by doing and the rewards are the accomplishments. Imagination and expressive language are core components in a student's individuality. Once individuality is honored, it becomes easier for teachers to introduce interdependent components of an educational system. As students begin to write, they soon notice that thinking, reading, and written composition are all systems.

Systems theory and written composition have not been blended in schools. A system is a cohesive conglomeration of interrelated and interdependent parts. Systems theory is the interdisciplinary study of systems. Due to inconsistent pedagogy, limited practice, and no clear system of composition instruction, many students suffer from the perils of poor writing skills and restricted literacy.

To improve a student's writing and speaking skills, the instructor must build lesson and unit plans that incorporate writing and speaking. Building the practices of consistent writing, reading, and speaking into all school disciplines fosters confidence and a command of language.

2
A RESOLUTION ON EBONICS

DONDA WEST WAS the lead writer of A Resolution on Ebonics at Chicago State University. She was instrumental in validating Black English as a form of cultural expression and as a language used by many African Americans. The document was written in response to the Ann Arbor decision and the amendment to the same decision (Martin Luther King Junior Elementary School Children et al. v. Ann Arbor School District). A few months after the Oakland Ebonics Resolution, the Chicago Resolution was passed unanimously by participants at the Symposium on Black English Vernacular/Ebonics at Chicago State University on April 3, 1997.

RESOLUTION

Members of the Chicago State University family and surrounding community, having discussed key issues related to Black English Vernacular also known as Ebonics, have reached and do hereby affirm the following conclusions:

1. Black English Vernacular (BEV) is a distinct variety of the English language spoken by most African Americans in the United States.

2. As a means of communication and cultural expression, BEV is a systematic and rule-governed dialect with valid syntax, morphology, semantics, and phonology.

3. BEV is so essential to African American cultural survival and prosperity that it needs to be cherished and celebrated by the whole African American community.

4. BEV is so influential in the lives of African American students that it can interfere with their academic performance. Therefore, educators should pay special attention to ways in which BEV can be used to help bridge the gap between the language many African American students bring to the classroom and standard American English.

5. Standard English is a language of wider usage, and so affirming the validity of BEV, teachers must make every effort to help students acquire standard English.

6. Educators and the public in general adopt and reflect perceptions and attitudes toward Black English Vernacular, however exceptions do exist according to demographics.

7. Scholars should be involved in further research and discourse to contribute to the continued clarification and validation of BEV.

8. Educational institutions should be informed of past, present, and future research on BEV.

9. The media has a responsibility to report, accurately, the issues related to BEV and,

10. All persons, African Americans in particular, regard BEV as a systemic, intelligent form of expression to be used along with standard English in communicating ideas.

To this day, Black English is misinterpreted in schools, courtrooms, and in business. Donda West was prescient with her thoughts on BEV, Systems Theory, and the ethic of care in public schools.

3

GENERAL SYSTEMS THEORY AND RHETORIC : TOWARD A NEW WORLD VIEW FOR TEACHERS OF WRITTEN COMPOSITION IN SECONDARY SCHOOLS AND COLLEGES

DONDA CLAIRANN WILLIAMS WEST completed her doctoral dissertation and earned the degree of Ed.D. from Auburn University on June 6, 1980. This was a turning point for her life as a scholar. Kanye was almost three years old and she had decisions to make about her career as a professor and researcher. Components from her manuscript on systems theory and rhetoric have been used in several school districts in the United States and abroad. Her dissertation was ahead of its time, and many of her discoveries remain relevant.

ABSTRACT

In 1979, after the development of many theories and methods in the teaching of written composition, the problems students have with writing clear and meaningful prose are still overwhelming. One reason for this unfortunate circumstance may stem from evidence that there is no consciously articulated world view shared by teachers of written composition that might serve as framework for teaching. In this work, General Systems Theory, is discussed as the most integrated theory investigated for possible world view and implications in the teaching of written composition. Selected research studies, theories, and strategies in written composition are presented and examined relative to general systems theory some of which are included in a systems approach to the teaching of writing suggested for teachers and students in secondary schools and colleges.

> There should be a consciously articulated world view of how to teach written composition.
>
> — DONDA RULE #1

ASPECTS OF THE SYSTEMS CONCEPT

For years, educators have been concerned about the difficulty students have in writing adequate and acceptable prose. From national writing tests, college placement examinations, college compositions, and high school essays, one can see severe limitations in the writing of an alarmingly large number of students.

If your children are attending college, chances are, they will be unable to write clear and cohesive expository text with any real degree of structure and lucidity. If they are in high school, planning to attend college, they are probably writing at a level far below the requirements of a first-year college student. If they are not planning to attend college, their skills in writing English may not even qualify them for menial tasks. And if they are attending elementary school, they are almost certainly not being given the kind of required reading material, much less writing instruction, that might make it possible for them eventually to write comprehensive English.

A number of reasons have been cited by teachers, linguists, and writers for this low achievement in writing. Some critics cite an apparent inadequate grounding in the basics of syntax, structure, and style; others place the blame on secondary school curricula that no longer require the wide range of reading students must have if they are to learn to write clearly.

Students need to be able to write clear and cohesive essays before entering college. Check the rigor of your child's school.

— DONDA RULE #2

THE NATURE OF THE STUDY

In an attempt to determine the most effective means of teaching written composition, researchers have investigated a number of possibilities. Some scholars and teachers have advocated the use of traditional grammar drills, a return to an earlier approach to teaching written composition; others are giving serious attention to exercises in transformational-generative grammar. T-unit lengthening, sentence combining, and rhetorical devices as possible means for teaching students to improve their writing. While some theories and approaches, both past and present, contribute significantly to the teaching of written composition, it appears that all of these methods are partial in that they fail to recognize writing as a total process.

Teachers of composition seem unable to develop a shared conceptual framework on which to base writing activities. Although important factors of writing are sometimes taught, they are usually taught in isolation from the composition as a whole rather than as interrelated elements functioning in particular ways for the good of the whole. It is erroneous to assume that competence in the structural/mechanical aspects of writing alone, or that knowledge about isolated factors of the composing process in itself, will yield a good writer.

However, many teachers of composition, having no comprehensive theory for teaching writing, continue to use such piecemeal approaches, making little progress in helping students solve the severe problems they have with written composition.

> Beware of teachers who have no theory in teaching composition and who teach writing as an isolated practice, and not an integrated one.
>
> — DONDA RULE #3

ALTHOUGH OTHER TEACHERS HAVE REALIZED THE PROBLEMS INHERENT in using such approaches, they still lack the unifying framework needed to teach writing. The purpose of this study then, is to formulate a theory for teaching composition that will allow teaching composition in a more integrated manner and to suggest ways in which such a theory may be implemented in the classroom.

Over four decades ago, a theory was introduced that was concerned with a more complete approach to viewing the many facets of our contemporary society. This theory referred to as "systems," "systems theory," or "systems view," emerged out of necessity when it was realized that a piecemeal predetermined approach to viewing scientific phenomena was no longer adequate and was even detrimental to the development of science. Defined in simplistic terms, the systems view is a way of looking at the world in terms of integrated relations. More specifically, a system can be defined as any phenomenon having interrelated parts that function as a complex of mutually dependent interacting elements as part of a larger whole.

Paul Weiss states that there are patterned processes which owe their typical configuration not to prearranged, absolutely stereotyped, mosaic of single-tracked component performances, but on the contrary, to the fact that the component activities have many degrees of freedom, but submit to the ordering restraints exerted upon them by the integral activity of the "whole" in its patterned systems dynamics.

The theory for teaching composition to be developed in this study is based on the assumption that the writing process lends itself to a systems approach in which integrated relations are more clearly noted and the composition is viewed as the product of a total process, rather than the binding together of fragmented parts. Such an approach demands initiative, creativity, and flexibility on the part of both instructor and student. A guide based on the concept of systems will be presented that reflects the belief that learning to write is an ongoing process that must not be hindered by prescribed and inflexible methods. Such an approach to the teaching of written composition requires the instructor to be more concerned with the actual progress of students than with a list of competency-based behavioral objectives. The very nature of writing suggests that such rigid, preconceived teaching methods may even hinder the progress of students in learning to compose effective prose. To establish a firm base from which to work in developing a comprehensive theory, it is essential that the general concept of systems be understood. The primary purpose of this first chapter is to present an overview of systems philosophies as they reflect various and sometimes conflicting attitudes about the nature of systems. Such an overview will form the basis for the development of a comprehensive theory in teaching written composition.

The Origin and Development of Systems Theory

The theory of systems has become an important foundation for the development within a number of disciplines. Many scholars have concerned themselves with the investigation, explanation, and use of a systems view of the world. The development of systems, systems theory, systems science, or one of several terms used to refer to the concept was necessitated primarily by the complexity of modern technology. Such an origin seems to suggest that systems theory is preeminently a mathematical field.

Ludwig Von Bertalanffy was one of the first to introduce the systems concept. His premise notes that systems theory is a broad view that far transcends technological problems and demands, a reorientation that has become necessary in science in general and in the gamut of disciplines from physics and biology to the behavioral and social sciences and to philosophy. It is operative, with varying degrees to success and exactitude, in various realms, and heralds a new world view of considerable impact.

Systems theory can be viewed from a number of perspectives and defined in a variety of ways. However, each way of looking at systems theory implies a new world view, a framework that deals with the complexities of wholes and the interrelationships that exist between elements of any particular system.

In further explaining the development of systems theory, Bertalanffy says technology has been led to think not in terms of single machines, but in those of "systems." A steam engine, automobile, or radio receiver was within the competence of the engineer trained in the respective specialty. But when it comes to ballistic missiles or space vehicles, they have to be assembled from components originating in heterogeneous mechanical, electronic, and chemical technologies. And these systems require precision and hardly any room for error. Whether traffic on the roads or in the sky, systems must be planned and arranged.

Thus, the systems approach became necessary. Ervin Laszlo, in *The Systems View of the World*, expresses many of the same concerns about systems theory as Bertalanffy. He notes that Western science regards a systems view or an integrated approach preferable to an atomistic one. He comments on the dangers of specialization without regard for whole systems.

Laszlo states that knowledge, instead of being pursued in depth and integrated in breadth, is pursued in depth in relative isolation. Instead of getting a continuous and coherent picture, we are getting fragments —remarkably detailed but isolated patterns.

> Fragmented thoughts should never supersede coherent thought.
>
> — DONDA RULE #4

Laszlo comments further on the problem of fragmentation and isolation and explains that "instead of looking at one thing at a time, and noting its behavior when exposed to one thing, science now looks at a number of different and interacting things and notes their behavior as a whole under diverse influences. As Laszlo states, "The systems view always treats systems as integrated wholes of their subsidiary components and never as the mechanic aggregate of parts in isolable causal relations.

In the *Structure of Scientific Revolutions*, Thomas S. Kuhn traces the development of scientific advancements with particular emphasis on the changes in world view. Kuhn points out several crises in the field of science that can be said to have resulted from an atomistic perspective rather than an integrated perspective held by the early scientists. He was careful to add, however, that such a perspective had been adequate for many scientific discoveries and was quite appropriate for the times.

Floyd W. Matson comments extensively on the development of science and the need for a more complete way of viewing the world. According to Floyd Matson, science has been slow in adopting new world views and has tended to cling to a mechanistic and deterministic perspective. Matson says that when tech advances, systems will affect one another.

Natural scientists were understandably reluctant to modify a framework that had proved so continuously fruitful both in theory and practice; not only natural scientists but social and political scientists as well were unwilling—and a substantial number remain unwilling today—to abandon a world view that, at whatever the price to human dignity and moral freedom, had brought determinate order and the illusion of certainty to the once-mysterious universe.

Matson further notes that such a fragmented way of viewing various phenomena in science is itself misleading, arguing that as scientists observe elements in isolation some distortion of reality is inevitable. He comments: the very attempt to observe a particle knocks it off its course, and the more accurately we pin down its position, for example, the more unsure we are of the degree to which we have affected its momentum. The same can happen in artistic works, where one note in a song can influence the rest of the song, another song, or an entire album. This interdependent system can also occur in writing.

> Discern relationships and situations, not isolated events. A system is a meal, not the recipe; a system is a song, not the notes.
>
> — DONDA RULE #5

Such an observation agrees with Ervin Laszlo's statement that "Newtonian science looked upon the physical universe as an exquisitely designed giant mechanism, obeying elegant deterministic laws of motion." Laszlo further explains that the specialist concentrates on detail and disregards the wider structure that gives it context. The new scientist however, concentrates on structure on all levels of magnitude and complexity, and fits detail into its general framework. He discerns relationships and situations, not atomistic facts and events.

PARTS AND WHOLES IN SYSTEMS

Not only has science undergone transformations that necessitate looking at the interrelationships and interdependence of elements as they relate to a whole, but the whole, unlike what the atomistic view may suggest, cannot be defined as simply the sum of its parts.

In *Parts and Wholes*, Daniel Lerner notes that functional wholes have been defined as systems "the behavior of which is not determined by that of their individual elements, but where the part-processes are themselves determined by the intrinsic nature of the whole.

What is distinctive of such systems is that their parts do not act, and do not possess characteristics, independently of one another. On the contrary, their parts are supposed to be so related that any alteration in one of them causes a change in all of the other parts. A change in the amount of an ingredient can change the taste, look, texture, and appeal of a food.

Lerner further asserts that functional wholes cannot be properly analyzed from an "additive point of view." The characteristic modes of functioning constituents must be studied in situ, and the structure of activities of the whole cannot be inferred from properties displayed by its constituents in isolation from the whole.

In the field of science, as in almost every other field, knowledge has often been gained through a piecemeal process that, no longer adequate. As scientists turn to a more encompassing way of viewing the world, so have scholars in other disciplines. As Laszlo states, "Those who believe that a patchwork approach is the only means of gaining a coherent and integrated world view today are mistaken."

He also comments that "we are beginning to realize the need for connecting the probes with one another and gaining some coherent insight into what exists." While Laszlo and others make the point that wholes are not simply irreducible to their parts and should not be studied as such, Benjamin Whorf goes further to point out that it is almost impossible to look at parts without affecting the whole (though the effect is not always readily apparent).

According to Whorf, "All real scientists have their eyes primarily on background phenomena and yet their studies have a way of bringing out a close relation between unsuspected realities.

Whorf's analysis supports the Lerner principle — wholes cannot have any part removed without altering both that part and the remaining parts of the system.

All of the aforementioned statements seem to point to some very important facts about a system or systems view. Most important, however, may be that any system must be explained in terms of its interrelated and mutually dependent parts that in themselves possess qualities of a whole. For example, a finger is in itself a system with its component cells, nerve endings, blood vessels, and so on. However, it is one of the five component parts needed to make a normally functioning hand. The hand can be seen as a system with a subsystem of fingers, thumb, and a palm making up a normal functioning hand. At another level, the hand can be seen as but one of several interdependent parts that make up a normal human body, another system.

If all of these parts are conceived of as separate parts working together in an integrated fashion for the good of the whole, then there is also a conception of the human finger, hand, and body of systems in and of themselves. Consider the particular manner in which these parts function together as systems and parts of a larger system. Beyond the pain and discomfort experienced in losing one of the parts such as the finger, it is essential that one consider what effect such a loss would have on the larger system (a 2 or 3 fingered hand). Indeed, a systems view involves all of these considerations. As Laszlo repeatedly points out, wholes cannot be simply reduced to the properties of their individual parts.

Laszlo uses examples extensively to emphasize the fact that wholes are more than the sum total of their parts and therefore are irreducible to the characteristics of each part. He maintains "it is quite possible that we could fully account for the properties of each whole if we could know the precise characteristics of all the parts and know all existing relationships between them. Then we could reduce the characteristics of the whole to the sum of the characteristics of the parts in interaction. But this involves integrating the data not merely for three bodies, but for three thousand, three million, three billion, or more, depending on the whole we are considering.

And since science cannot perform this feat even for a set of three parts, it is quite hopeless to think that it can do it for any of the more complex phenomena it comes across in nature or man. Laszlo further illustrates this point, noting that characteristics of groups tend to be preserved even if their individual members change.

Laszlo proposes that athletic teams exchange their players, with younger ones replacing the veteran performers. Yet the teams usually maintain much of their own characteristic, their tactics and techniques, their fighting spirit, and so on. Such wholes are complex systems and to reduce them to parts is not only inadequate, but a gross distortion of the concept of systems.

Systems versus Mechanistic View

In applying the systems concept to the living organism, Paul A. Weiss also attacks the mechanistic framework that dominated the thinking of scholars before the introduction of systems theory.

According to Weiss, "The necessity becomes compelling to accept organic entities as systems subject to network dynamics in the sense of modern systems theory, rather than as bundles of micro-precisely programmed linear chain reactions." He continues by saying that a strictly mechanistic, machine-like, notion of the nature of living organisms presupposes a high degree of precision in the special and chronological program according to which the innumerable concurrent chains are composed and arrayed.

Weiss repeatedly explains his disfavor regarding a mechanistic predetermined perspective and notes flaws that arise from such thinking. Weiss comments specifically on the thinking of Jacques Loeb, who describes animal behavior in terms of "rigidly concentrated reflex sequences" and who, in the words of Weiss, "epitomizes the kind of mechanistic preconception." According to Weiss, not only had that mechanistic thinking become outdated in physics, but studies of actual behavior of animals showed none of the presumed stereotypes in the manner in which animals obtained their objectives.

Weiss continues his explanation by pointing out that even though the predicted results, were often achieved, the steps in achieving such were highly complex, diversified, and not predetermined.

> Fluidity can be an asset as long as the system accommodates. If the system is fluid and open, the possibilities are endless.
>
> — DONDA RULE #6

THE HIERARCHIC STRUCTURE OF SYSTEMS

Arthur Koestler says that hierarchy is fundamental to systems theory. Hierarchic organization is used organization of any system. All complex structures and processes of a relatively stable character display hierarchic organization, and this applies regardless of whether we are considering inanimate systems, living organisms, social organizations, or patterns of behavior.

Parts of a system are systems within themselves functioning as quasi-independent wholes. Koestler refers to such subsystems as autonomous holism.

A "part," as we generally use the word, means something fragmentary and incomplete, which by itself would have no legitimate existence. There is a tendency among holists to use the word "whole" or "Gestalt" as something complete in itself. But wholes and parts in this absolute sense do not exist anywhere, either in the domain of living organisms or of social organizations. What we find are intermediary structures on a series of levels in ascending order of complexity, each of which has two faces looking in opposite directions: the face turned towards the lower level is that of an autonomous whole, the one turned upward is that of a dependent part.

Although Koestler carefully emphasizes the idea that the term *hierarchy* should not be used in systems to refer to order of rank of on a linear scale, John H. Milsum explains hierarch of systems in just that manner. Milsum sees a rigid hierarchical structure that he believes to be apparent in many highly developed animal societies.

Unlike Koestler, who recognized the existence of an underlying hierarchical structure in systems. Milsum points out how everyday language and folklore are full of expressions implicitly involving the hierarchical concept, for example, "knowing one's place," "climbing the ladder," "the delicate balance of nature," and "the food pyramid." Even the long history of political struggle has largely been aimed at producing revolutions which only replace one hierarchy with another; indeed, the relatively recent democratic movements and revolutions aimed at establishing ideal egalitarian societies have, from the functional viewpoints of how power flows and how control is exercised, resulted in only slightly modified hierarchies.

Milsum's view of the underlying hierarchical structure of a system also suggests a rigidity not found in Koestler's explanation. This is reflected in Milsum's view that a hierarchical society is under vigorous attack because of its perceived rigidity and consequent hampering of man's efforts to realize himself fully.

Politics have no real power to help the most vulnerable an oppressed people because they are regulated by faulty hierarchies.

— Donda Rule #7

On the contrary, Koestler does not view the hierarchical structure as limiting but as an orderly structure that allows for unlimited growth and development because of the autonomous nature of each holon.

Top-Down hierarchy is inferior when the braintrust at the bottom is never allowed to express and share. Rejecting hierarchy is sometimes the best method for growth.

— Donda Rule #8

The idea that a hierarchical structure is apparent in systems is discussed from a different perspective by Jerome S. Bruner in "On Voluntary Action and its Hierarchical Structure." Bruner emphasizes the belief that "many biological systems operate from the outset as hierarchically organized wholes by their very nature." He says that some systems achieve such structure slowly and with caution. In early human growth, the initially well-organized systems seem to be predominantly of the automatic or "over-controlled" type—as with breathing, swallowing, and initial sucking. With a minimum of initial priming, all three of these are potentiated easily embedded smoothly into a larger context of action.

Bruner explains that biological systems have natural hierarchical structures involving systems at various levels, and these levels function independently as well as interdependently. He views this as a natural kind of organization agreeing with Koestler's concept of the holon and seeks to describe rather than to prescribe its behavior.

Systems Theory in Various Fields of Study

The concept of systems has been approached by scholars with

varying attitudes and beliefs about the theory. The social scientist has been as interested as the psychologist; the biologist as interested as the mathematician; the humanist as interested as the gestaltist. Bertalanffy comments that even the politician has come to regard the systems concept as important. He notes that a Canadian premier described a systems approach in his platform as an interrelationship between elements and constituents of society. The essential factor in public problems, issues, policies, and programs must always be considered and evaluated as interdependent components of a total system.

It is necessary to study not only parts and processes in isolation, to solve decisive problems found in the organization.

This belief is reflected by social scientist Lawrence K. Frank. For a unified theory of human behavior, we need a conceptual framework enabling us to recognize many dimensions of human behavior as observed in the cultural, social, and geographic environments. This calls for a concept of the organism's personality — whose varied behavior we are seeking to understand.

> Problems are interdependent components. Solving them may take a holon (whole/part) approach.
>
> — DONDA RULE #9

Frank is concerned with the interrelationships and interdependence of man in his environment. Rather than viewing humans as isolated individuals responding to particular stimuli in cause/effect relationships, Frank views man as an integral part (and whole) of society.

Human conduct and feeling as circular, reciprocal, transactional, occurring between and among persons. All the varied patterns, rituals, institutional practices, and symbols of group life appear as different modes of communication. But each person can approach, negotiate, and seek meaning through interpersonal and interpersonal social dynamics.

Man is a part of society and the whole society.

— DONDA RULE #10

A less unified theory often fails to recognize important factors about individuals and the society of which they are a part. In his prefacing remarks. Roy Grinker, editor of *Toward a Unified Theory of Human Behavior*, emphasizes that the behavior of individuals is not understandable apart from the culture of which they are a part, and culture cannot be understood without considering the individuals in it.

It used to be the general trend of psychology to reduce mental happenings and behavior into a bundle of sensations, drives, innate and learned reactions, or whatever ultimate elements are theoretically presupposed. In contrast, the system concept tries to bring the psychophysiological organism into the focus of the scientific endeavor, says Bertalanffy.

The theory of systems can be viewed as a most comprehensive concept. It allows for the total development of any living organism as it attempts to understand the natural order of interrelated phenomena rather than to prescribe it.

The systems concept is essential to the further development of man and his surroundings. As pointed out by R. L. Ackoff almost 20 years ago, we have witnessed the emergence of the "system" as a key concept in scientific research. Systems have been studied for centuries, but something new has been added. . . . the tendency to study systems as an entity rather than as a conglomeration of parts is no longer to isolate phenomena in narrowly confined contexts, but rather to open interactions for examination and to examine larger and larger slices of nature. We are participating in what is probably the most comprehensive effort to attain a synthesis of scientific knowledge yet made.

Seek to understand, not to prescribe.

— DONDA RULE #11

The foregoing discussion of major ideas regarding the concept of systems seems to have a number of implications for those who have struggled to find a comprehensive theory from which to draw strategies for teaching students to write acceptable prose. It may well be that a new conceptual theory is needed in the area of composition instruction in much the same way that a new conceptual theory was needed in science and other fields.

Writing should approached from a holistic view.

— DONDA RULE #12

Most composition teachers correct students' papers. Instead, they should encourage a closer examination of the composition's body, meaning, and syntax.

— DONDA RULE #13

A number of single factors about the teaching of written composition have been examined in some depth. Many of them can be instrumental in helping students to improve their writing. But if significant development is to occur in the writing ability of students, the writing process must be viewed from a holistic perspective from the outset. Both instructor and student must view the composition itself as a whole achieved only through the ordering of many interrelated and interdependent parts. First, however, it will be important to review how the systems concept has been applied, and in some instances misapplied, in education. Such is the purpose of the chapter that follows.

4
SYSTEMS APPROACHES AND EDUCATION

IN THE SEARCH for more effective ways to improve the quality of education, a growing number of educators are investigating the concept of systems. No longer are these educators content with many of the more traditional theories, especially those that fail to provide a means for viewing and understanding problems encountered in today's schools. Many of today's educators have come to regard the utilization of systems approaches as not only useful, but crucial to the development of better educational practices. Advocates of systems approaches argue that if the educational institutions are going to be able to meet the challenge of fostering the growth of each student, an open-ended and integrated approach is essential. While many who support a systems approach agree that it is by no means the answer to all of the problems in education, they regard such an approach as essential, primarily because it provides the much needed avenue for viewing phenomena from the broadest perspective, a need that is becoming increasingly important in education.

With the growing interest in the concept of systems in general, systems approaches are being discussed in many educational publications as scholars from various fields continue to proclaim the usefulness, inclusiveness, and timeliness of systems.

John L. Hayman notes, that such terms as "systems approach and systems analysis" have appeared more and more in the educational literature in recent years, and we are likely to see more of them as time passes.

The Need for Systems Approaches in Education

Recognizing that many factors must be considered in order to implement any program, teach any subject, or assess any problem accurately, educators are continually demonstrating their commitment to systems approaches.

Systems approaches imply a holistic and comprehensive problem-solving approach. In trying to increase reading ability in schools, teachers would not look merely at the reading instruction received; they would examine all factors which influencing reading ability, and they would identify a reading "system" and examine it from the perspective of general systems theory.

This requires more effort than we are accustomed to investing in particular problems. However, the failure to approach problems from this perspective accounts for much of our frustration. Due to budget and time constraints, teachers tend to be piecemeal and shortsighted in their efforts, and they oversimplify instruction. This hurts the student. Obviously, we must learn to be more effective, and this will require a systems approach.

> Schools that segregate all learning locales compromise the potential of disciplines.
>
> — Donda Rule #14

> Teachers aren't paid enough to do triage and more acute evaluation of students' works. Due to large class sizes, they settle for correcting papers, offering no reflective behavior from the student.
>
> — Donda Rule #15

Like Hayman, Randall believes "an educational system must appreciate the perspective of the pupil." They speak of an instructional system in advocating the, systems approach and defines an instructional system as that part of the learner's environment which is purposely controlled by an instructional institution so as to secure by that learner the attainment of specified learning objectives. While Randall acknowledges the need for structured learning situations to achieve specified goals, he focuses on the needs of students and makes clear the fact that learning is effected in many ways.

According to Randall, systems must be learner-centered. Specifically, that means that it must avoid being either classroom-centered or even school-centered, for the very obvious reason that it is not only what goes on in the classroom or the school that effects changes in pupils.

> Systems theory is a road sign for Kanye's artistry. He learned the rules of hip-hop, R&B, soul, rock, jazz, folk, classical, the blues, beat production, and mastered the Ensoniq ASR-10. After learning the rules of hierarchy, he broke them and embraced a new set of systems.
>
> — DONDA RULE #16

The terms "system," "instructional system," and "educational system" have appeared with increasing frequency in the literature. In addition. something identified as the systems approach has been invented or discovered which apparently holds great promise for the solution of complex education and training problems.

Silvern, Randall, Hayman, and an increasing number of educators have recognized the implications of systems approaches for education and they are fully convinced that such approaches can be used for the improvement of educational practices. Although still in their infancy as a recognized means of improving education, systems approaches are becoming more widespread as the need for change and growth in education grows.

James Hoetker notes, systems thinking is only beginning to

encroach on education, but it has become a preferred mode of investigation in academic disciplines from anthropology and economics to psychology and zoology. "Systems thinking" may be valuable simply because it can help us see old things in new ways, prompting us to ask new questions. Systems approaches help us to discover what we do not know.

> Education reforms are 10 years behind social, cultural, and technological changes. Most reforms are a burden and waste of time.
>
> — DONDA RULE #17

The concept of systems appears to offer approaches to the solutions of problems in a rapidly changing society, and many scholars are adopting systems philosophies in an attempt to enhance educational solutions.

Educational reforms traditionally are very burdensome enterprises to a nation. They are stretched out and occur at intervals through the history of a nation. The harmful consequence is that the educational system for long periods of time is quite out of synchronism with on-going developments and transformations which characterize a continually and rapidly changing society.

We are just beginning to understand that continual changes in a society as a whole should be paralleled—perhaps even to some extent directed—by a well-planned, systemized and continuous revision of the entire educational system. The educational system has to learn to live with change.

Erikson suggests that educators have a common tendency to hold tightly to their already established ideas about education even when there is need for change. He views systems approaches as both timely and effective for education.

Leland Wooton states, "If we are to deal effectively with the challenges of today, it seems clear to me that we cannot expect to solve our problems by focusing on them within the perspective of the past." Perhaps the most difficult task facing educators today is that of asking a set of questions which are more relevant to our problems. It is my belief that systems analysis or the systems approach can provide some of the answers we need to deal with the weaknesses of our present system.

> Today's teachers cling to the obsolete. This is tragic for students.
>
> — DONDA RULE #18

Anthony G. Oettinger finds the systems approach invaluable in education because of the emphasis that is placed on the interrelationships of parts in order to understand the whole. The systems approach is a new philosophy of education, a new commitment to human values, and finally, a new awareness that our present institutions of education are incapable of adopting technological environments.

> Educational systems should drive society, not follow it.
>
> — DONDA RULE #19

THE SYSTEMS APPROACH AND VARYING PERSPECTIVES

In many instances, students are expected and required to achieve predetermined goals set forth in the program as teachers implement rigidly planned curricula and pedagogy insisting on the use of behavioral objectives. Such a view of this systems approach is also apparent at the administrative level, as administrators, adopt rigidly planned programs to deal with budgetary and other problems. Such programs may be used effectively, but they cannot be looked at as it complete implementation of a systems approach.

A number of special "tools" are used in the application of system theory, and use of these tools is often mistakably identified as the systems approach or as systems analysis. A planner may make a PERT chart (Program Evaluation Review Technique) to outline his intended activities, pronouncing himself engaged in systems analysis. A finance director may begin installation of program budgeting, and may be considering himself to be following the systems approach. What they are really doing is using tools which have been developed as a part of systems methodology.

Hayman sees value in many of the tools that have been developed from the broader framework of systems, but to him they are just tools, only single parts of the larger system.

Educators focus on single components, not realizing the need for diverse methods of instruction.

Lately, instructors have become enamored with computer assisted instruction, self-paced study, or some other individual method. This has been perhaps the major failing of the process of innovation in education. Despite much jawboning to the contrary, very seldom has a very detailed look been taken at the existing courses in today's curricula. If this were done, the rudimentary fact would be noted that most courses are composed, and rightly so, of diverse types of material which meet multiple learning objectives. It follows, then, that diverse learning methods should be applied in each course to enable students to best comprehend the diverse material.

Like Rockart, Gabriel D. Ofiesh sees new technology as crucial in implementing the systems approach in education. Ofiesh contends, that there is an acute awareness that the crowded classrooms, the split shifts, and all the other undesirable yet expedient measures which were forced upon schools to meet today's needs will be totally unacceptable tomorrow. To continue the traditional system, in which individualized attention has become a rarity, could ultimately force us to limit educational opportunity to a "choice" segment of the population.

Advocating a more effective approach, Ofiesh adds, "The rapid accumulation of information in almost every discipline and endeavor has forced the field of education to search for new methods of acquiring, assembling, analyzing, and disseminating information."

Rapid information accumulation should force the creation of new methods.

— DONDA RULE #20

The systems approach to education" in brief, involves the specification of objectives, the assessment of student repertories, the development of instructional strategies, testing and revision of instructional units (validation), and finally packaging and administering a validated learning system. This approach results in the development of learning experiences for students, which are adjusted to students' learning modes.

Several educators have joined Ofiesh and Rockart in hailing technology and new media as vital tools in applying the concept of systems in education. But approaching the problem from different perspectives, some have defined the use of a systems approach in broader terms. E. W. Martin notes that the concept of a "system" is getting noticed in both industrial and academic circles. While Martin does not view the systems approach as education's panacea, he does view it as an extremely helpful approach. Martin says, "The system concept does not provide a set of rules for solving all problems, but it is a useful device for viewing many phenomena."

When we attempt to understand complex systems, problems arise at two distinct levels: the micro level (understanding the basic cause-and-effect relationships governing the performance of the almost elementary subsystems) and the macro level (understanding the effect on systems performance of the complex chains of interrelationships between the elementary subsystems). Historically, we have been able to cope reasonably well with the micro problems by isolating them, studying them in some detail, and building models incorporating the relationships).

Some of our difficulties in attempting to educate people are closely related to these macro systems problems. We can teach individual subjects, but the student frequently cannot integrate his knowledge to form an understanding of the total organization. Each course, for example, represents a subsystem when viewed as a part of the larger whole. But it is itself a system within which other subsystems exist.

The general way of defining the systems approach is to view it as a way of looking at a process, a methodology that enables us to analyze a complex problem and then to synthesize a solution. This process is an interdependent process since it is composed of the sum total of separate parts working independently and in interaction to achieve previously specified objectives. The education process is thus viewed as a system and its components would be teaching and instruction, management and administration, facilities and support, community and learners, and an array of other components depending on how "open" we define our system. Each of these when considered alone could be considered a separate system; however, when put together each part become a subsystem of the overall system.

Although the systems approach has been analyzed in different ways, perhaps the most fundamental concept of it is summarized by John L. Hayman who, believing Bertalanffy's description of systems to be most complete, used it as the basis for applying the systems approach to education.

Hayman states, "The systems approach itself is a problem solving process or set of processes applicable at various levels in education . . . the systems approach is powerful and appears capable of systematically producing change. It has proven these qualities in applications in other fields, and it almost certainly has an important role in the future of education."

Counselors, teachers, and educational technologists believe it timely and vitally important to institute the concept of systems in education. But before presenting specific ways in which the systems approach is being used in education, it should be clearly understood that skepticism of the systems approach has been exhibited by some educators.

The humanistic critics see education as an "open-ended" affair, and they do not trust the advocates of systems approaches to have the skill, imagination, or patience to deal with dynamic, indeterminate systems.

They find systems people to be pre-occupied with technology and cost effectiveness, unwilling to give more than lip service to the validation of objectives or the real complexities of human learning.

In further assessing the attitude of humanistic critics, Hoetker says many humanistic critics fear that systems technology will be used only to reinforce the oppressive, dehumanizing tendencies of present-day schools and to destroy the saving remnant of genuinely humane and authentic relationships between teachers and pupils that have somehow managed to survive.

Hoetker argues that systems approaches have been viewed in a number of ways and that in some instances they have been and will probably continue to be misused.

Systems technologies can be put to humanistic uses; they will be used to reform the tools or to devise more effective replacements for them. The tendency of currently dominant systems experts to rate political and dollar costs as more important than human costs is probably assessed accurately by the humanistic critics.

> A limited system can hurt you; an open system can benefit everyone.
>
> — DONDA RULE #21

Also looking at a systems approach with some skepticism, Harry J. Hartley presents what he considers limitations of the systems approach. Hartley notes a number of limitations and all of those listed are goal distortion, cult of testing, and cult of efficiency.

Hartley states that there is an unfortunate tendency to place greater emphasis on those goals such as cognition mastery, and to neglect more important goals that cannot be quantified and measured, such as moral perspective.

Organizing education in terms of the economic theory of input and output is rather dangerous when our evaluation methods are so primitive. It tends to minimize those significant school activities, especially in the affective—moral—esthetic realm that do not lend themselves to the crude testing instruments available. Testing based on poor instruments, disputable assumptions, and incorrectly interpreted or purposely manipulated data can offset the advantages of systems procedures.

Hartley also comments on the disturbing effects of what he terms the cult of efficiency factor in using systems approaches. Emphasis on economic saving through systems analysis may be at the expense of accomplishing. The need exists in local schools for occasional uneconomic allocations of resources. In this way, schools will benefit from money being "wasted" on noneconomic values that mirror our social conscience.

Such limitations seem to indicate further how the systems approach can be misinterpreted. The most desirable approach would be without such limitations in that primitive evaluation procedures, for example, would not be used, but all possible alternatives would be examined so that learning could be evaluated appropriately. Although Hartley views systems approaches as being limited in a number of ways. This listing of shortcomings of systems analysis, offered by one who is strongly committed to the systems approach, should not be interpreted as a rejection of the emergent techniques. It is my opinion that these limitations are far outweighed by the potential advantages to be gained.

> Standardized tests are crude and cruel.
>
> — Donda Rule #22

In the final analysis, the success of systems procedures is dependent on the artistry of the user. Even with the dissent of some educators regarding the systems approach and the differing and sometimes conflicting attitudes about the systems approach, are rapidly gaining popularity in today's educational circles. As several have stated, the systems approach is by no means problem free, but when implemented as a total process in which learning is encouraged, problems can be minimized and learning increased.

. . .

The Use of Systems Approaches in Education

Systems approaches in education have been implemented in various ways. Some have used a standard packaged curriculum as a system of approaching learning. Others have developed personalized learning programs and have suggested that these approaches are the better way of instituting the concept of systems in education.

In stating the necessary conditions for learning, Dewey's beliefs may be parallel to those of Hayman. Dewey says learning requires judgment and art to select from the total circumstances of a case, what elements are the conditions of learning, which are influential, and which secondary or irrelevant. It requires candor and sincerity to keep track of failures as well as successes and to estimate the relative degree of success obtained. It requires trained and acute observation to note the indications of progress in learning, and even more to detect their causes—a much more highly skilled kind of observation than is needed to note the results of mechanically applied tests.

Presenting similar conditions for learning in a more structured form, Hayman notes that five steps are needed. Specifically he notes these steps: (1) identifying the problem, (2) analyzing the system, (3) stating goals and objectives, (4) identifying and evaluating options, and (5) synthesizing the system. Hayman explains each step in detail noting that although step one, identifying the problem, may seem obvious, difficulty often arises even in this first step because the problem is not always thoroughly identified. Roger A. Kaufman cautions that some people select, produce, and implement solutions before the problem has been identified and substantiated, though it is essential that the problem be clearly defined and understood to achieve the desired results. Finding solutions to problems and discovering the cause of learning are an an endless process. In some urban schools, teachers and administrators think they know the problems before getting to know the culture, neighborhood, the students, parents, and political climate of the school district.

Step two, systems analysis, involves looking at the current system, its parts, and their interrelationships. After viewing the current function of the system, it is then necessary to conduct a needs assessment. This step is extremely important in approaching learning-related problems. The needs assessment helps make apparent the problems that must be overcome in a given learning situation.

The final stage in analyzing system entails defining constraints so that solutions suggested will be possible to achieve. Hayman states, "In identifying constraints, one examines the resources available—money, personnel, facilities, and the like—and determines their status."

The third step, stating goals and objectives, is vitally important according to Hayman. He notes, setting goals and objectives is not just a matter of determining the current area of interest among the target audience at different levels and in different locations, and deciding on the basis of realistic expectancies. The values and desires of the target audience and of relevant others such as parents and the broader community must also be taken into account, reaching consensus.

Identifying and evaluating options, which Hayman defines as the fourth step in applying the systems approach in education, involves deciding on the most affective way to achieve the desired results. He states:

There will always be a number of alternative ways in which the desired outcomes might be achieved. The problem is to pick the one which is most likely to succeed best in the system which has been analyzed and described. Making decisions requires knowledge of the relevant characteristics of each alternative, and here it is essential that theory, past results, and practical experiences be brought into play.

The final step in implementing the systems approach in education is systems synthesis and evaluation. This step involves putting together what seems to be the optimum solution on the basis of all information gathered in the assessment of the total system. One must also be concerned with how the proposed system fits into an even larger system.

No system or procedure is ever the ultimate system. A particular system like any other tool should constantly be challenged, evaluated, and should be revised or rejected other tools are more responsive and offer greater utility. While Hayman presents the theoretical basis for the use of the systems approach in education, and suggests ways for its implementation, others have instituted specific programs that from their perspective, represent the systems approach.

John C. Flannigan presents a program entitled Project PLAN in an attempt to provide a more comprehensive view of education and to implement a systems approach. Project PLAN, a Program for Learning According to Needs, represents a comprehensive system of education designed to make full use of available knowledge and resources to provide the full development of potentials of all young people.

The five functions of Project PLAN, which are:

1. Learning about educational and occupational opportunities, citizenship roles, and the nature of other activities involving self-expression, appreciation, and personal realization and satisfactions.

2. Formulating personal values and evaluating personal potentials.

3. Learning to make wise decisions.

4. Planning personal development.

5. Learning to manage a personal development program.

Flannigan explains that Project PLAN encourages students to take responsibility for their own educational and personal development, beginning in the first grade. Several types of materials and procedures are used in the Project that are determined by the needs and abilities of students. These materials and procedures began with specific educational objectives, information, and skills to be achieved. Students are evaluated to determine whether or not the objectives have been achieved. Flannigan points out that such a program would replace current educational procedures in which a student is required to conform to administrative lock-step and the whims of specific teachers.

Describing more specifically how a systems approach has been applied in education, Launor F. Carter discusses its use in the development of an introduction to reading program for Mexican-American children. The developers of the program, Ralph Melaragno and Gerald Newmark, thoroughly investigated the needs of the students and proceeded to find effective ways to meet their needs. After much research, it was found that a number of factors affected the reading abilities of the Mexican-American students. A few of which include the paucity of vocabulary background, poor listening skills, pronunciation problems, and poor language habits that resulted in speaking in single words and fragments rather than complete sentences.

Language use does not determine intellect.

— Donda Rule #23

When a reading test was administrated to obtain some idea of the reading level, the mean score was 13 for the Mexican-American children and 52 for the Anglo children out of a possible score of 71. Another test was administered—the results of which indicated that there were no differences in the general intellectual capabilities of the students. After more research, it was found that Mexican-American children could not understand "direction" words such as top, bottom, fewest, identical, largest. etc., and without an understanding of these, frequently used in reading and in other instructional materials, students had great difficulty in acquiring reading skills. Several techniques were employed in order to get the children to master the 10 words considered most important. Some of these techniques were as follows: asking teachers to teach the words in whatever manner they could, having teachers to break the class down into three small groups, using student pairs (pairing students who understand the words with students who did not), using special workbooks and tape recordings (the technique most effective for the largest number of students), and teaching parents or other family members the tutoring process. All the above techniques were tried and revised until a system for teaching the Mexican-American students could be developed. The system involved stating the need, defining the objectives, defining constraints, identifying alternatives, selecting the best alternative, testing, evaluating, and modifying. There were numerous factors involved in developing the system, and each had to be explored carefully. The results showed that only two of 50 students failed to master all 10 words.

Not only is the systems approach being considered as a viable means of facilitating instruction such as the teaching of reading, but its usefulness has been argued in other areas of education as well. T.

Antoinette Ryan advocates the use of a system approach in counseling and counselor education. Professionalization cannot be attained in counselor education programs that continue to treat selection, coursework, practicum, and on-the-job counseling as unrelated, independent element, rather than as articulated components of a unified system.

General systems theory gives a framework for making such an approach and systems techniques provide tools whereby viable management decisions can be implemented in integrated, interrelated, unified programs of counseling and counselor education.

Ryan discusses the details of implementing the systems approach in counseling and counselor education noting many of the same steps involved in previous discussions. Noting both advantages and limitations of systems techniques, Ryan concludes that increased effectiveness of counseling and counseling education systems can be achieved by applying techniques aimed at achieving greater wholeness, stronger interrelationships, more capability and greater optimization using systems techniques.

In addition to such areas as counseling, teaching, administration, and technology, the systems approach in education serves other important functions. Clifford H. Edwards explores the possibilities of community involvement in a systems approach to curriculum. He notes a growing demand by various groups for significant input into decisions made in an attempt to improve education and to eradicate the competition for power and control. Edwards says systems approach is recommended as one alternative that may help reduce the propensity various groups have for seizing power and encourage a sharing of control and responsibility.

Edwards points out several problems in education that result from power struggles and lack of input from important sources and designs the approach to facilitate integration of ideas and pooling of efforts. Rather than being placed at odds with one another, various groups are organized so as to be mutually dependent upon one another. If they are mutually independent, then it does little good to operate in isolated autonomy.

Edwards sees such a systems approach as most effective when "one individual is not responsible to any other particular individual, but rather is globally responsible to everyone in the system including teachers, administrators, parents, and students.

> Individuals are responsible to groups; groups are responsible to individuals.
>
> — Donda Rule #24

All participants in the system should contribute on the same basis to further the goals of education. Then members of the community can make viable contribution, without having to struggle for and obtain power first.

> Unchecked power interferes with outcomes.
>
> — Donda Rule #25

Even though many questions are still being raised regarding the use of the systems approach in education, the general concept of systems has numerous implications for education. The future of the systems approach in education looks bright. The systems approach has been viewed as a way to stimulate community involvement, develop counseling programs, improve administrative operations, teach reading and other subjects, encourage individualized instruction, and to assess the total process of education. When properly used, the systems approach is invaluable and can be implemented in ways that will produce astounding results.

Although in recent years, systems approaches have been recognized to some extent in the field of English instruction, and have been applied from various perspectives by English teachers, the consistent and effective use of such an approach seems to have suffered because no adequate theory, no integrated theory has been developed. A look at the current practices in teaching writing, seems to indicate a need for further investigation of how more integrated techniques might aid in facilitating development in that area. Many researchers and instructors in written composition and rhetoric have already made important discoveries about teaching writing as they have explored individual facets of the writing process. In the chapter that follows, selected research studies and current theories concerning the teaching of written composition will be reviewed. It is believed that important aspects of these theories can be integrated and used in the context of systems, helping to yield the development of an integrated and comprehensive systems theory for the teaching of writing.

5

RESEARCH AND THEORIES IN THE TEACHING OF WRITTEN COMPOSITION

For decades, English instructors at all levels of education have tried to find effective ways to teach students how to write adequate prose. Concomitant to these efforts, a number of theories and attitudes about teaching written composition were developed. Some teachers believed that the mastery of traditional grammar was the most essential aspect of learning to write correctly and effectively; others believed that the development of thinking processes was most essential. Some held rigidly to the notion that constant practice in writing would bring about the desired results, and still others claimed that it was not the frequency of student writing but the quality of teacher evaluation that produced the greatest improvement in student writing.

> When you focus on grammar only, the meaning may be obscured.
>
> — Donda Rule #26

As a result of the differing philosophies and attitudes regarding the teaching of writing, and in an attempt to determine the most effective teaching methods, a number of research studies have been conducted in written composition. While some of these studies may have contributed to more effective instruction, the current status of writing not only in today's schools, but in society at large indicates an urgent need for attention.

In recent years, several major studies have been conducted that dealt with some aspect of written composition both at the secondary and college levels. These studies have revealed interesting and important facts about the teaching of writing, but for justifiable reasons, many of them have received severe criticism. According to Braddock, Jones, and Schoer, research in the area of "larger elements" of composition, not merely with grammar and mechanics), have not been frequently conducted with the knowledge of and care one associates with the physical sciences. Today's research in composition may be compared to chemical research as it emerged from the period of alchemy: some terms are being defined usefully, a number of procedures are being refined, but the field as a whole is laced with dreams, prejudices, and makeshift operations.

This assertion, made almost two decades ago in reference to earlier studies in written composition, still applies to much of the more current research in the area. Although the research has presented some valuable information about teaching writing, in many instances, the total, or as Braddock states, the field as a whole, has not been examined closely, and only partial solutions have been offered. It is this kind of research that makes even more apparent the need for an integrated approach and an integrated theory for the teaching of written composition.

Not enough investigators are really informing themselves about the procedures and results of previous research before embarking on their own. Two few of them conduct pilot experiments and validate their measuring instruments before undertaking an investigation. Too many seem to be bent more on obtaining an advanced degree or another publication than on making a genuine contribution to knowledge. . . . and far too few of those who have conducted an initial piece of research follow it through with further exploration or replicate the investigations of others.

> Prejudice and inconsistent instruction can devastate a student's progress.
>
> — DONDA RULE #27

Braddock says composition research is not highly developed. If researchers wish to give it strength and depth, they must re-examine critically the structure and techniques of their studies.

Most of the studies conducted, however, dealt with factors that could be easily measured such as the length of sentences or the use of various rhetorical constructions. Thus, factors such as the creative or productive thinking processes have received little attention in experimental research. Not all known or assumed factors can be dealt with adequately in any single study or course, but researchers have yet to integrate and examine the interrelationship of many of the individual factors found to influence writing ability in order to develop the broader framework that is needed in writing instruction. Instead, separate bits of information have been offered, some of which, if integrated, could ultimately contribute to the development of a comprehensive program for teaching writing.

> Composition instructors focus on sentence length and rhetorical construction rather than the thought process and meaning.
>
> — DONDA RULE #28

A review of selected research studies in written composition makes clear the current findings. Such a review is an initial step in integrating information needed for developing a comprehensive theory for writing.

SELECTED RESEARCH STUDIES IN WRITTEN COMPOSITION

In 1953, Gerald Kincaid investigated the writing behavior of students enrolled in a first quarter college English class to see if his hypotheses were correct that: (1) any assigned topic provides the same stimulus as any other topic, (2) any topic elicits constant responses at different times, (3) the psychological pressure of taking an examination has no adverse effect an the quality of writing, and (4) the quality of student writing is stable from topic to topic and from time to time with or without exam pressure regardless of writing ability. Important variables were controlled, and procedures were carefully applied in examining some 320 papers written in situations that made it possible to test the hypotheses. The results show that as a whole, the average quality of student writing was not affected by the topic assigned or the conditions under which topics were assigned. Also, the psychological pressure of taking an exam did not adversely affect the quality of student writing. The study revealed however, that for individual students, the quality of writing did appear to be affected according to day-to-day writing consistency.

Objective tests were administered to all three groups, but there was no significant difference in student performance on these tests. Several findings resulted from this study. It appears that better students were the better writers. Nonetheless, pressure of final examination conditions did not appear to affect either the better or worse writers. The quality of the worse writers did vary according to the mode of discourse.

From the Kincaid study came a number of implications for instructors who teach writing. Again, it is understandable that only a few of the factors that affect writing ability could be investigated in the one study, but other factors and their relationship to the whole must be considered in drawing final conclusions about the teaching of writing.

A study was conducted by Earl W. Buxton to determine the relative effectiveness of regular practice in writing and of two methods of teaching writing: (l) a freedom from restraint writing method and, (2) a prevision, writing, and revision or revision method. Buxton found that students in the revision method group (the most demanding method in that students were expected to write on the assigned topic and to revise papers that were strictly and thoroughly graded) improved their writing very significantly over students in the control group and significantly over students in the writing group. Students in the latter group, whose papers were not strictly graded but merely commented upon, were permitted to select their topic and were not required to revise. The three groups did not differ significantly in their gain on the two objective post-tests but did differ significantly in their gain on the posttest essay examination. Clearly, it seems that objective tests may not be used to measure changes that may be measured by essay examinations. Results also show that thorough grading and the requirement of students to revise their papers aid significantly in improvement in writing.

Ronald J. Harris raised still another question regarding the teaching of composition in his study completed in 1962. Harris investigated the relative effectiveness of two teaching methods in teaching writing to students aged 12–14: (l) the formal grammar method and (2) the direct method. Students in the formal grammar method group studied and applied the terms of formal grammar in composition work, whereas the other students used none of these terms and devoted the time saved to direct practice in writing.

The formal grammar group was instructed in the parts of speech and were taught traditional grammar lessons. The direct method group used no textbook or grammatical terminology and were taught by means of "example and imitation" as the instructor pointed out errors in compositions. Again, the procedures used in this study were quite involved as Harris sought to control as many variables as possible and to provide appropriate situations for eliciting information about the two groups. Harris found that students in the direct method group improved considerably in their writing ability and as a result of the low achievement of students in the formal grammar group, he wrote said that low achievement may be seen as a major factor throwing doubt on the advisability of studying formal grammar in the early part of the secondary school.

Harris included students from a variety of backgrounds and thus concludes that the failure to profit from instruction in traditional grammar is thus not confined to any one educational environment or category of children.

Since students in the direct method group improved considerably while students in the formal grammar method group showed little improvement and in some cases regressed, Harris concludes, "It seems safe to infer that the study of English grammatical terminology had a negligible or even a relatively harmful effect on the correctness of children's writing."

As the teaching of traditional grammar continually failed to be a sufficient solution to the problems students encountered in writing, researchers began to look at other factors that they believed might positively influence students' writing ability. They also sought to explore the aspects that seemed to be indicative of acceptable prose. In 1965, Kellogg Hunt analyzed writing samples of fourth, eighth, and twelfth grade students and adults in search of grammatical trends in the frequency of various grammatical structures written by the students. Hunt analyzed a number of factors including sentence length, clause length, and subordination ratio. He concluded that the T-unit (defined as one main clause plus the subordinate clauses and phrases attached to or embedded within it), was the most significant index of writing maturity. Thus, Hunt used the T-unit to establish a norm against which teaching effectiveness could be measured.

In 1975, Linda Brooks developed an experimental curriculum for teaching the cumulative sentence at the seventh-grade level. Following the overall design of the O'Hare study, the purpose of the Brooks study was to measure the relative teaching effectiveness of the experimental treatment on the writing ability of seventh grade students.

Specifically, Brooks was interested in measuring the growth in syntactic maturity of 73 students in the control group and comparing it to the growth of the 76 students in the experimental group. The students whose IQ scores ranged from 75 to 138, and of whom 29 percent were black, were taught by three junior high school teachers, each teaching one control and one experimental group. The experimental group studied the cumulative sentence for 1.5 hours per week for 30 weeks and were exposed to four kinds of sentence modifiers: noun clusters, verb clusters, adjective clusters, and nominative absolutes. For the same length of time, the control group followed the regular seventh grade curriculum. Students in both groups wrote for 40 minutes on three separate occasions. The samples were then analyzed for measures of syntactic maturity and for the occurrence of sentence modifiers.

The results of the study show that the experimental group who studied the cumulative sentence, showed no more growth in syntactic maturity than students in the regular curriculum. Although the experimental group did produce significantly more noun clusters and verb clusters than the control group, they did not produce a significantly larger number of adjective clusters and nominative absolutes.

The Brooks study raises some questions regarding teaching generative rhetoric as early as grade seven. While the general consensus is that in 1966, Donald Bateman and Frank Zidonis attempted studying how the cumulative sentence can be helpful to students, the experimental curriculum used in the Brooks study indicates that it is more appropriate for somewhat older students (9th and 10th graders). In the two-year study, students who were taught transformational generative grammar did improve their writing significantly. Bateman and Zidonis relate several findings and draw as a major conclusion that "a knowledge of generative grammar seems to enable students to reduce the occurrence of errors in their writing."

In 1969, Mellon used sentence combining patterns based on transformational grammar to teach students to write better prose. He too found that students who were taught to combine sentences improved significantly in their writing even though no formal study of transformational grammar was undertaken.

Four years later, Frank O'Hare completed work that was based on earlier studies in transformational grammar and in sentence combining. O'Hare argued that the more informal approach of sentence combining was far more effective in teaching writing than a formal study of transformational grammar. He further believed that the formal presentation of the generative grammar might inhibit the development of students. Students were divided into both control and experimental groups with those in the experimental group receiving instruction in sentence-combining. The results showed that students who practiced sentence-combining exercises, showed a great improvement in syntactic maturity and that their essays were usually preferred by the instructors.

As a follow-up to the studies conducted by Mellon and O'Hare, Warren E. Combs researched further effects of sentence-combining practice on writing ability. The purpose of the study was to test whether, 1) syntactic maturity gains achieved by the Mellon and O'Hare procedures were replicable with a seventh grade population, and, 2) if syntactic maturity gains were retained as measures by a delayed post-test of students' free writing.

The overall quality of the writing of students receiving sentence-combining practice will be judged superior to that of students not receiving sentence-combining practice as measured by an expanded matched-pairs design.

Combs used as subjects, 100 white students from a suburban Minneapolis junior high school with a considerable range of abilities. These students comprised four classes (two experimental classes and two control classes). Two experienced junior high English teachers executed all the activities and each teacher was assigned a control group and an experimental group to control for teacher effect. The writing exercises were synchronized and all students completed the same number and kind of exercises. The literature of varying genres was taught during the interval between testing periods and the teachers also exposed students to activities involving word skills, dictionary skills, punctuation, and spelling. Students received practice in taking the STEP writing test. There was no formal instruction of grammar and there were no class discussions that required a knowledge of it. Teachers used Mellon's *Our Sentences and Their Grammar* as a source book in addition to examples suggested by O'Hare. The basic transformations practiced by O'Hare's students were practiced by the students in this study. Time spent with the sentence-combining exercises was about the same in all three studies (Mellon's, O'Hare's, and Combs'). No reference was made to transformational grammar; instead, simple sentence-combining techniques were introduced and plenty of time was allowed for practice.

Two kinds of measures were used to assess the effect of the treatment. Students' compositions were analyzed to determine the mean number of words per T-unit and words per clause. A panel of teacher-raters rated the quality of students' writing at pre- and post-test to assess the effect of sentence-combining practice on judgments of writing quality, the system of forced choice between matched pairs of students' papers was employed. Seven teacher-raters rated the papers. They had no intimate knowledge of the O'Hare study and were unaware of the purpose of their analysis. They used a number and letter system to identify the papers, and read them at random to judge the relative quality of each pair of compositions.

> Students who can combine sentences show syntactic maturity. Sentence combining exercises have a direct, positive effect on middle school students' writing.
>
> — DONDA RULE #29

The results of the study confirmed the hypotheses that significant gains in syntactic maturity achieved and retained in the experimental group was distinctively superior to that of the control group. It should be noted, however, that the three studies suggest considerable variation in growth and that an erosion or a decline in syntactic maturity was revealed by the delayed post-test (the erosion being about one-half of the gain).

Nevertheless, it can be generally concluded from this study that sentence-combining practice has a positive effect on the writing of seventh graders.

Whereas most researchers in written composition focus their attention on the written product itself, one researcher, Janet Emig, concentrates on the composing process and investigates such factors as the students' feelings, attitudes, and self-concept. Emig uses a case study method in a very thorough investigation of the writing process of selected twelfth grade students. Such an approach, that of a case study, is not a common practice among researchers in written composition. In the Emig study, eight twelfth grade students of average or above average ability were selected from various secondary high schools in Chicago, ranging from an all white upper middle class suburban school to an almost all Black urban school. Emig asked the students to give autobiographies of their writing experiences and to compose aloud three themes with a proctor, while being recorded. From an analysis of the students' accounts and their writing behavior, Emig concluded that twelfth-grade writers engage in two modes of composing—reflexive and extensive—characterized by processes of different lengths with different clusterings of components. These differences can be ascertained and characterized through having twelfth-grade writers compose aloud—that is, attempting to externalize their processes of composing.

In the composing processes of twelfth-grade writers, an implied or an explicit set of stylistic principles governs the selection and arrangement of components—lexical, syntactic, rhetorical, and imagaic.

For twelfth-grade writers, extensive writing occurs chiefly as a school-sponsored activity; reflexive, as a self-sponsored activity.

Emig points out the need to distinguish between the two modes of discourse, reflexive and extensive stating,

"The reflexive mode focuses on the writers' thoughts and feelings concerning their experiences; the chief audience is the writer himself . . . the style is tentative, personal and exploratory. The extensive focuses upon the writers conveying a message or a communication to another; the style is assured, impersonal and often reportorial."

In four sessions with each of the eight subjects, Emig recorded (both on paper and on tape) the responses and behavior of the students. She provides a detailed account of her findings as a result of such investigation noting specifically the behavior, feelings, attitudes, and abilities of the students. Unlike most researchers, Emig is concerned with those aspects that are not easily measured or that cannot be measured at all. This passage from Emig's conclusion about the writing process of one of her subjects indicates a concern for the students as persons rather than mechanisms in the act of composing. She records,

"Lynn seems to write with greater ease in the extensive than in the reflexive mode. There seems to be both personal and curricular reasons. Personally, she seems reserved about her feelings, although open, even volatile, about ideas. It could even be said she reveals a certain fear of feeling. Also, the curriculum she has experienced in composition both in elementary and in secondary school, has provided her with very few school-sponsored opportunities for engaging in reflexive writing, as her writing autobiography and a review of her theme folders confirm."

Based upon the behaviors and reports of the eight students used in the study, Emig was able to comment on factors she calls the components of the composing process. They include: the context for a given process of composing, nature of stimuli, prewriting and planning, starting, composing aloud, stopping, contemplating the product, reformulation, and the seeming influence on writing by teachers of composition. General findings are as follows:

Twelfth graders in this sample engage in two modes of composing —reflexive and extensive—characterized by processes of different lengths with different clustering of components. For the twelfth graders in this sample extensive writing occurs chiefly as a school-sponsored activity. Reflexive writing is a longer process with more elements and components than writing in the extensive mode.

Reflexive writing has a far longer prewriting period; starting, stopping. and contemplating the product are more discernible moments, and reformulation occurs more frequently. Reflexive writing occurs often as poetry; the engagement with the field of discourse is at once committed and exploratory. The self is the chief audience or, occasionally, a trusted peer.

Extensive writing occurs chiefly as prose: the attitude toward the field of discourse is often detached and reportorial.

Adults, notably teachers, are the chief audience for extensive writing. While Lynn points out that "so much remains unexamined about the composing process of children, youth, and adults, and admits that the generalizations about the composing process of twelfth graders would be more valid if the sample were enlarged. Her study has a number of implications for teachers of written composition. Emig concludes that teachers of English under-conceptualize and oversimplify the process of composing.

> Teaching composition can be a neurotic activity. Keep your classroom writing instruction as fluid and flexible.
>
> — Donda Rule #30

Planning degenerates into outlining; reformulating becomes the correction of minor infelicities. They truncate the process of composing. In most American high schools, there is no time provided, and no place where a student can ever be alone, although all accounts of writers tell us a condition of solitude is requisite for certain kinds of encounters with words and concepts. At the other end of the process, revision is lost. not only because it is too narrowly defined but because, again, no time is provided for any major reformulation or reconceptualization . . . Much of the teaching of compositions in American high schools is essentially a neurotic activity. There is little evidence that the persistent pointing out of specific errors in student themes leads to the elimination of these errors, yet teachers expend much of their energy in this futile and unrewarding exercise.

> To write with quality, you need to be comfortable being alone.
>
> — Donda Rule #31

Clearly, the Lynn study reflects an awareness that the process of writing is at least as important as the finished paper itself. It is this kind of broad perspective that is needed in the teaching of writing.

The studies summarized above examine some aspect of composition that may be regarded as essential. The Lynn study, which appears to be broadest in scope, addresses a number of concerns as a process, rather than a product. It seems that each study should be considered in light of all that is known about the teaching of writing and that the interrelationship of parts and wholes as they relate to the teaching of writing need be brought to the forefront. Instead of formulating a theory on the basis of Hunt's findings or on those of Bateman and Zidonis, or on any single attempt at improving writing instruction, each study should be examined for its contribution to the larger whole. Systems thinking has been overlooked when any known aspect of writing instruction is not viewed in relationship to the whole.

> Correcting errors does not lead to the elimination of errors. Teachers must model good writing and allow students to find their own errors.
>
> — DONDA RULE #32

THEORIES IN THE TEACHING OF WRITTEN COMPOSITION

Theories for the teaching of written composition have been developed by scholars and teachers for centuries. Since the fifth century BC, when a theory of rhetoric was possibly introduced by Corax of Syracuse to help ordinary men plead their case in court, men have been seriously concerned with effective communication. Even in the fifth century BC, before the development of rhetoric as written discourse, rhetoricians developed theories that some believe are applicable to writing instruction today. Perhaps the most thorough investigation of classical rhetoric is that of Edward P. J. Corbett who links aspects of rhetoricians.

Aristotle hoped to show that rhetoric was not, as Plato had accused it of being, a mere "knack," but was a true art, a teachable and systematic discipline that could guide men in adapting means to an end. With his philosophic treatise, Aristotle became the fountainhead of all later rhetorical theory.

Rhetoric, first conceived of as a persuasive art, has come to encompass much more than it did in the Fifth century BC. However, writing is still thought of today (as Aristotle said of classical rhetoric) as a systematic discipline that has great value for students.

It important for students to develop mechanical skills in writing, but equally important for them to develop thinking skills. This premise was also held by the earliest rhetoricians. In other words, what is said is equally as important as how it is said, and teachers encourage students to think critically and to write responsibly. Noting the concern of early rhetoricians about the content of a composition Corbett says Quintilian insisted that in addition to being intellectually fortified for his office, the orator must be trained to be a man of strong moral character. It was this insistence on the intellectual and moral training of the aspiring orator that made Cicero and Quintilian the two most potent classical influences on rhetorical education in England and America.

It is necessary to develop a theory or rationale from which to teach, then to offer exercises based on the theory, and finally to have students imitate the writing of accomplished writers. It was and still is believed that a sound theory with appropriate exercises is essential and that through the imitation of effective writers, students can become more proficient in their own writing.

Frank D'Angelo comments generally on the revival of rhetoric and notes the revival of rhetoric has led both to a significant interest in the possibilities of classical rhetoric as well as to a growing interest in the development of new rhetorics. Those who are interested in the revival of classical rhetoric feel that it can still be the basis of a valid approach to writing and that it offers the only complete system of rhetoric that is available to us today.

Edward P. J. Corbett says the elaborate system of the ancients, which taught the student how to find something to say, how to select and organize his material, and how to phrase it in the best possible way, is still useful and effective—perhaps more useful and effective than the various courses of study that replace it. No system, classical or modern, has been devised that can change students suddenly and irrevocably into masters of elegant prose. But the ancient teachers of rhetoric, refusing to be impressed by the notion of "creative self-expression" until the student had a self to express and a facility for expressing it, succeeded in large part in developing a method which, when well taught, could help students to write and speak effectively.

Know yourself and get grounded.

— DONDA RULE #33

Although Corbett and others place great validity in the revival of classical rhetoric as a basis on which to proceed in teaching written composition today, an impressive number of scholars tend to disagree. They argue that modern approaches are more important than the techniques offered by the ancient rhetoricians.

Wayne Booth says practicing daily forms of persuasion authors never dreamed of, we inevitably hunger for a theory that will do justice to our rhetorical experiences, and we find that the categories used by earlier theorists do not quite do the job.

Other weaknesses in classical rhetoric are pointed out by Richard Young and Alton Becker. They start by saying the classical art of invention stressed authoritative confirmation of present beliefs, while modern modes of inquiry stress imaginative discovery of new facts and relationships. Second, the art of arrangement includes only patterns of persuasion, and neglects consideration of form in other important rhetorical modes such as description, narration, and exposition. Third, both the art of arrangement and the art of style are divorced from content — failing to consider the importance of the art of discovery in the shaping of form. And finally, the art of style is concerned primarily with embellishing, clarifying, and giving point to sentence, an approach which neglects both the deeper personal roots of style and the ways in which style is manifested in patterns beyond the sentence.

Young and Becker, who are more apt to point out the limitations of the ancient philosophies, there are scholars who see the solution in the integration of both the old and the new. Such scholars see clearly the need for modern concepts as well as for the recognition of older ones.

Frank D'Angelo says no new rhetoric can afford to neglect the rhetorical concepts of invention, arrangement, and style, or such traditional basic concerns as the relationship of the writer to his purpose, his subject, and his audience. One might conclude that rhetoric does not necessarily end with Aristotle, but this is not the reason some of concepts associated with Aristotle cannot be used as a point of departure.

Further, D'Angelo states his belief that "the best new rhetoric is one that will somehow relate the old and new in rhetoric."

Some of the modern philosophies regarding the teaching of written composition reflect a variety of new and hopeful beliefs and attitudes. More and more, those concerned with teaching writing are finding effective ways to encourage students to learn how to write. Still, information is disseminated in bits and pieces which often are in need of a larger context to be most effective. One important view is presented by Roger Sale, who believes that "writing can be learned but it cannot be taught." Sale points out fallacies when writing is taught as a mechanical process rather than learned as a more total process that serves as a means to greater ends.

Sale says, "Writing cannot be taught, because it is not a teachable series of actions or patterns, it is the sketch that tells the world and ourselves who we are. The student who begins to see the real limits that his teacher has, no matter how good or bad that teacher may be, can also begin to see what he might then do on his own. It would be nice to think we could talk about writing without talking about being a teacher and being a student, but, in fact, most writing in America today is untaught writing, in classes, with teachers. Given that, it seems that the best thing to do about "getting" or "making" the writing better is to ask about the relationship between teacher and student, and to insist that most of the writing that is done is bad because the relationship is mechanical or unreal to the student. When that relationship is one of power and acceptance of power, writing can be taught no better than the writing machines can do. When that relationship is one of real question, real answer, and real possibility, writing cannot be taught at all. But it can be learned."

Sale's theory differs drastically from those who say that teaching mechanical skills is the sole or primary factor in teaching writing.

Further, his theory indicates an awareness of systems thinking as it is applied to writing instruction. Sale does not abandon completely some of the more traditional concepts, however, he talks extensively about organization, style, usage, and grammar. Integrated into a larger framework for teaching written composition, Sale's contributions are most significant.

Hans P. Guth advocates a synthesis of some already existing ideas.

He notes several kinds of rhetoric including: (1) the rhetoric of order, a conservative rhetoric concerned with order, structure, organization, coherence, unity, clarity, exactness, accuracy, precision, and simplicity; (2) the rhetoric of discovery concerned with open-mindedness, skepticism, tentativeness, flexibility, diversity, and dialogue; and (3) the rhetoric of confrontation concerned with commitment, engagement, relevance, solidarity, and defiance. Guth comments at some length on each of these types stating specifically the strengths and weaknesses of each. He posits at conservative rhetoric of order stresses the structure of the product. A liberal rhetoric of discovery stresses the integrity of the writer. A radical rhetoric of confrontation stresses impact on the audience. With a slight rearrangement, we can make them part of a larger scheme in which we focus on the major elements of the communication process.

James Sledd comments extensively on the need for a new perspective in teaching writing, noting how traditional theories have in some ways been detrimental, while more modern theories, specifically theories based on linguistics, have not only been an asset, but an essential factor in teaching students to improve their writing ability. Commenting on the inadequacy of traditional theory, Sledd notes that the usual teaching about clauses rests on the false assumption that grammatical and semantic categories do coincide. Sledd urges writing instructors to adopt a linguistic perspective.

Confrontational rhetoric makes the audience think.

— DONDA RULE #34

The first and most important way in which linguistics can serve us as teachers of composition is that it can help us see what we have to do, and how we can best do it. The teacher who knows some linguistics sees the composition course in light of his knowledge; and if he does not foolishly conclude that linguistics is a panacea, his introduction to linguistic science may be part of a general reorientation which is more valuable than anyone specific use of linguistic methods or materials.

Sledd points out specific ways in which knowledge of linguistics is helpful to the teacher of composition including as an example how linguistics makes apparent the relationship between speech and writing. Linguistics can teach us something about the relations between speech and writing—for example, that speech comes first in time and in importance, that writing is an incomplete but partially independent secondary representation of speech, that the kinds of speech that we normally write are very different from plain talk, and that mastering these differences is a large part of our students' job.

Speech requires urgency; writing requires contemplation.

— DONDA RULE #35

Even though Sledd views the linguistic; approach to teaching composition as more productive than traditional approaches, such an approach in itself, is not the total solution to the problem. But as part of a larger whole or a broader framework, one that incorporates a number of significant findings about writing instruction, the ideas suggested by Sledd could be put to greater use.

Expressing concern for students' inability to write well-formed sentences, Richard Graves outlines a strategy for teaching sentence meaning. Graves points out that a writer lacks understanding of (and therefore skill in using) English sentences, and second, he lacks understanding of how such sentences are put together to form paragraphs. Until these two matters are solved, he is not likely to show much improvement in written expression, no matter how much grammar he is taught (traditional, transformational, or whatever) or how much he is drilled in usage or cajoled to change his dialect. Some may object that this solution may seem too obvious, yet an examination of the paper reveals that most of its failures occur at the sentence level.

Graves, like the advocates of systems approaches, argues that "in order to be successful, the strategy must take into account the learner's present level of knowledge; it must begin where he is. Graves outlines strategies for understanding all types of sentences and notes that the young writer should be encouraged to make sure that every sentence has something to say. Step-by-step he gives a detailed description of how instructors may go about aiding their students in the development of writing clear, meaningful, and honest prose, commenting in-depth on how students may be encouraged to develop style. This vivid picture of sentence sense may be invaluable to instructors who find that their students continually fail to write complete well-formed sentences.

Graves states that until the fragments are expanded and filled out, until the redundancies are eliminated or combined with something else, until the whole thing is taken apart and put back together in good English sentences, then all other corrections are just so much tinkering and so much window dressing.

Speaking and writing are tools to convey meaning.

— Donda Rule #36

Francis Christensen believes that "if the new grammar is to be brought to bear on composition, it must be brought to bear on the rhetoric of the sentence." Thus, he developed a generative rhetoric of the sentence, and later, a generative rhetoric of the paragraph. He agrees with many in the field that although writing instructors expect students to produce effective writings, they do not really teach students to write. Further, Christensen believes that what is needed is "a rhetoric of the sentence that will do more than combine the ideas of sentences, but one that will generate ideas." Christensen points out four principles that he believes to be essential in developing such a rhetoric: (1) addition, (2) direction of movement, (1) levels of generality or levels of abstraction, and (4) texture. The first principle, addition, is based on Christensen's belief that greater meaning is made in the writing by adding as opposed to subtracting and that meaning is achieved through adding words to the base noun, verb, or main clause. He states that the foundation for a generative or productive rhetoric stems from a process of addition.

About direction of movement, Christensen notes that modifiers are added before or after a noun, verb, or clause, and giving them a flowing and ebbing movement. After discussing these structural principles of addition and direction of movement, Christensen describes the two principles of meaning: levels of generality and texture. He points out that the main clause of a sentence is likely to be stated at the broader level of generality, at which point the forward movement of the sentence is stopped as the writer moves to lower levels of generality. Texture, says Christensen is that quality provided by descriptive or evaluative terms and may be considered thin or rich depending on the writer's use of such terms.

Perhaps there is more involved in the acquisition of good writing skills than is addressed in Christensen's rhetoric. Even though Christensen feels that ideas are generated in this kind of rhetoric, the extent to which a student applies creative thinking is not considered or discussed.

Approaching rhetoric or the teaching of composition from a linguistic and relatively involved point of view, Richard Young and Alton Becker explain Kenneth Pike's tagmenic theory and the possibilities in such a theory for the teaching of writing. Pike, a linguistic scholar, had sought to determine whether linguistics could provide the basis for a method of improving competence in writing. Many linguists and composition teachers had assumed that it could, yet the actual contributions of linguistics had not borne out the assumption. New methods of grammatical analysis and pattern practice, and sophisticated approaches to punctuation and usage—to name some of the more significant contributions—came nowhere near providing the basis for a coherent and comprehensive method. Pike suggested that one particular linguistic theory, tagmemics, could make a much more extensive and fundamental contribution by supplying the theoretical principles and problem-solving procedures necessary for a distinctly new approach to rhetoric.

Essentially, the tagmemics theory involves looking at the process of writing from various perspectives, especially the trimodal theory of particle, wave, and field. Viewing for example, a flower from this perspective. Young and Becker say that a particle description of a flower emphasizes features that make it distinctive from other flowers. A wave description emphasizes the flower as a moment in a process from seed to final decay (even this is only a peak in a larger wave) or as merging into a scene. A field description may partition a flower into its functional parts or classify it in a taxonomical system.

Young and Becker further emphasize the idea that one can view a topic trimodally and soon discover a wide range of significant perspectives. A tagmemic rhetoric stands somewhere between the rigorous theories of science and the almost purely intuitive theories of the humanities. We see no reason to reject the insights of either the former or the latter, believing that all new knowledge—like the process of writing itself—involves both intuitive analogy and formal precision.

The tagmemic rhetoric attempts to synthesize old and new ideas about rhetoric, conservative and radical attitudes toward rhetoric, and theoretical thinking and practical application of rhetoric. However, it might best serve the purposes of rhetoric, or of the teaching of composition, when viewed as part of a larger framework, or perhaps expanded to include, more directly, other factors that concern the writing instructor.

Frank D'Angelo posits that we have barely touched upon the possible concerns of a new rhetoric. It seems that anyone interested in developing a new approach to rhetoric must go outside his field to consider recent studies in linguistics, semantics, psychology, and literary criticism, to name just a few areas of interdisciplinary concern. Composition is an organic development that begins with a kind of intuitive grasp of the end to be achieved and that concludes when that end is brought to completion. The problem of composing is the problem of how an intention or purpose that is already partially realized in the mind gets what it needs to complete itself. The metaphor that perhaps best describes this process is that of a tree whose potential is already clearly realized in the seed. The seed is like the gestalt in the process of invention. It contains within itself everything necessary for a mature development, but unless it is given careful attention and nourishment, it may never reach fruition.

D'Angelo also points out that the relationship of elements to the whole (or of a sentence to a total composition, for example) and the interrelationships of elements must be considered in developing a theory that will be comprehensive enough to account for a variety of occurrences in the writing process.

One of the most important features of the conceptual theory of rhetoric, is that it seeks explanations for what is observed at some deeper level of reality. Another important characteristic of this theory is the importance it gives to wholes to the logical priority of the whole over its parts. The whole and its parts can be explained satisfactorily only in terms of particular relationships that exist among them. This viewpoint does not deny that the sentence and the paragraph have important structural characteristics of their own. But the sentence and the paragraph are more important as they relate the complex network of relationships that link them to the longer discourse.

> Writing is to be understood by the reader. The writer should not be selfish.
>
> — DONDA RULE #37

D'Angelo's comments clearly reflect the systems concept. Unlike Christensen, who points out only the generative nature of both sentences and paragraphs, D'Angelo is concerned about the larger whole. Similar to the tagmemic theory, the conceptual theory of rhetoric focuses on the writing process as a phenomenon that is multi-dimensional and in need of a broader framework. Rhetoric seems to be badly in need of a new organizing principle, a new conceptual framework which will not only relate the old and new in writing, but which will also produce a fairly coherent body of ideas about the nature of the written language.

In an essay on style and rhetoric, Edward Corbett notes that style has been a concern of rhetoricians since the beginning of rhetoric in Fifth century Athens. Using bibliographical sources, Corbett traces the history of style and comments on its treatment in various works, he includes in the discussion an article by Louis T. Milic entitled, "Theories of Style and Their Implications for Teaching Composition." Here, Milic presents three basic theories of style: (1) the theory of ornate form of rhetorical dualism (the theory that claims a separate existence for form and content, dressed in a variety of outfits), (2) the individualist or psychological monism (style is the man), and (3) the organic theory, the Crocean aesthetic monism, which denies the possibility of any separation of content and form.

Milic contends that the first theory should be embraced in order that composition might be taught in the classroom. In the college composition course, which represents for most students their first formal training in rhetoric, an awareness must be instilled of the existence of alternatives, of different ways of saying the same thing, of the options that language offers.

This belief on the part of Milic regarding the teaching of form and content raises serious questions in the minds of those who advocate a systems philosophy. Such dualism does not take into account that even though at one level both form and content exist separately, they are inextricably bound and that one can have no meaning without the other.

> Form and function drive rhetoric. Making sense without style can bore the reader. All style and no sense leaves the reader with folly.
>
> — DONDA RULE #38

The Tate compilation is an invaluable source for the teacher of composition as it also includes such rhetoricians as Frank D'Angelo and Mina Shaughnessy and such topics as linguistics, rhetorical analysis, and dialects. The articles included further define writing as a process that entails an infinite number of possibilities that must be regarded and integrated in order to facilitate better writing.

Mina P. Shaughnessy discusses several problems encountered by students who have difficulty with such basic tasks as composing a clear sentence or spelling a word correctly. She deals specifically with teacher expectations and notes that handwriting and punctuation, syntax, spelling, and vocabulary must all be looked at objectively in the teaching of written composition. Nevertheless, Shaughnessy is concerned about the problems of the individual student and advocates a student-centered curriculum for all who enroll in a writing class. She notes that programs are not the answer to problems students have with writing, but that teachers are. She comments further that there is no easy way to teach writing effectively.

Starting by noting the essential part that handwriting and punctuation play in the composing process, Shaughnessy proceeds to discuss the types of errors that the basic writing student makes in syntax. Consolidation, blurred patterns, and inversions are types of errors students commonly make in syntax. Some of these errors are made because they have not internalized language patterns, some because they do not know how writers behave, and some because they lack confidence and are fearful of the writing process. Using verbs appropriately appears to present the most difficulty for the basic writing students. They also have difficulty with nouns, failing to use the necessary inflection or to indicate possession. Shaughnessy notes that in dealing with such problems, the curriculum must be individualized and that the students' dialect is an important aspect to consider.

In her discussion on spelling and vocabulary, Shaughnessy notes types of errors made and offers suggestions for improvement. A spelling error may result from an unfamiliarity with the structure of a word, lack of experience with a word, reversal of a letter, or the use of a homophone for the word intended. Nonetheless, accurate spelling is essential for effective writing and an adequate vocabulary makes possible more options for the writer. As Shaughnessy notes, words learned well clarify and extend meaning and thus better enable students to elaborate, compare, condense, define, allude, and express themselves more fully. Shaughnessy, in her concern for helping students to minimize the problems outlined here, considers not just the problem itself, but the reasons it may exist. Defining the problem accurately, the first step in a systems approach, is perhaps the most important. If a student's difficulty in using the appropriate inflection stems from his dialect, then as Shaughnessy insists, dialect must be considered, understood, and treated as a part of the solution to tile problem.

> Don't be afraid of verb use. Fear of verbs becomes fear of action. And if you're afraid to write proactively, your writing compromises power.
>
> — DONDA RULE #39

Where Shaughnessy isolates the errors made by the basic writing student in order to deal with the errors more effectively, she does not isolate them as totally independent of the essay as a whole. This in-depth study of errors and expectations in written composition helps to put into perspective some specific problems students have with composing prose and offers practical suggestions for one who views a systems perspective as a viable alternative in teaching written composition.

In *The Nature of Literature*, William F. Irmscher, points out how literature functions as an art form and how one might go about writing on literary topics. Irmscher discusses such topics as the meaning of literature, literary criticism, and the influence of literature. He comments extensively on the characters, action, setting, form and structure, thought and meaning, and the language in various forms of literature. It is the influence of literature, however, that serves as the basis for most of Irmscher's comments. He notes that through characters, literature reveals human motives and invites identification and reaction. Good literature reveals man in conflict and it objectifies experience so that it can be viewed and contemplated.

Irmscher exhibits a keen awareness of what literature is, how it serves to stimulate writing, and how it is interpreted and treated by writers. In noting a few general approaches that might be used in writing about literature, Irmscher comments that one can summarize, interpret, analyze, and evaluate. He includes nine examples of writing done by college students in response to literature and his comments about the student papers further reflect his agreement with some systems advocates that many elements work together to produce the more important whole, that prescription can be defeating, and that self reflection is essential in learning and in writing.

Examples of writing indicate that writing about literature is within the capability of any thoughtful person . . . that there is no stereotype for the theme about literature. In fact, prescribing any kind of model would defeat the main theme of this composition. Given some understanding of the elements that go into making up literature, you have to find the best way you possibly can to make clear your own understandings and feelings. In fact, in the process of writing about literature, you may find that you have come to know yourself in a more meaningful way.

Writing can be your mirror. Let it be your mirror.

— DONDA RULE #40

It is the ultimate objective of the teacher who approaches writing from a systems perspective to encourage and insist on self-reflection. Further, since the systems curriculum is student-centered, it must have the personal development of the student, a goal of searching for self.

In a discussion on the development of a philosophy of composition, E. D. Hirsch begins by stating that we must first dispel that myth that writing is merely a secondary representation of speech. Hirsch discusses the issue of standard and non-standard language arguing that students should be taught the grammar of standard English not because it is linguistically accepted, but because standard English is not likely to change significantly in grammar or phonology as are other dialects. Hirsch paints out, however, that "oral speech follows linguistic rules that are no less rigorous than those of any literate language. To assert, then, that any oral dialect is 'incorrect' is to state a linguistic prejudice that has no foundation in linguistic fact."

Every dialect follows its own rules, and every competent native speaker of the dialect speaks it correctly. Correctness is an internal feature of a particular dialect, not an arbitrary feature outside it. This kind of scientific inquiry into the nature of language and dialects is essential to the teaching of writing from a systems perspective. Our failure to search for and find the truth regarding diversity in language and the function of dialects has contributed to a legacy of linguistic prejudice and kept us prisoner to methods that were virtually ineffective for many students.

Another concern expressed by Hirsch is that of increased communicative efficiency. Hirsch points out that the trend to achieve the same effects with less and less reader effort is becoming more and more prevalent. This brings up the question of readability discussed in the latter half of Hirsch's work. Relative readability is discussed as a stylistic principle that might serve as a basis for judging the stylistic excellence of prose. Thus, one must question the implications readability may have in formulating a philosophy of composition.

Oral dialect is correct if the listener understands the speaker.

— DONDA RULE #41

Hirsch comments on the limiting nature of some of the textbooks and practices of some writing teachers. More specifically, he states, "One of the great drawbacks of practical composition handbooks is their unreliable and speculative character owing to the limited research on which their advice is based. The present state of our knowledge, the more detailed the advice the more likely it is to be wrong."

Realizing that we must approach the subject of written composition from a broad rather than the historically limited perspective, Hirsch, congruent with the systems philosophers, holds that an understanding and ordering of many underlying facts and factors ranging from the spoken language to the use of handbooks, is essential in the development of an adequate philosophy of composition.

In *Research and Composing*, a compilation of articles on the teaching of writing, editors Charles Cooper and Lee Odell, comment on the limitations of basic assumptions still held about writing today. They point out that a number of studies seem to indicate that many conventional assumptions about the teaching of writing are not borne out by an analysis of expository writing. It appears that many researchers have assumed that the most significant kind of question was what materials and procedures will improve students' work in written composition? Thus, the primary task becomes to determine the effectiveness of specific instructional materials and procedures, rather than finding out exactly what information and skills teachers and researchers ought to be concerned with.

Cooper rand Odell stress that the basic problem in writing is discovering what one wishes to say, not simply deciding how best to present ideas that already exist, fully formulated, in one's mind.

Because past research and theories in composition have sometimes failed to reflect an adequate understanding of the composing process, several writers have presented what they consider a more adequate understanding of the process of writing. In addition to Charles Cooper and Lee Odell, others, among whom are Cynthia Courts, James Britton, Richard Young, and Donald Murray, present ideas and raise new questions about the nature of learning and teaching writing. In one article, Cooper, Odell, and Courts have as their main concern a new set of assumptions about discourse that might serve to replace outdated ones. These writers cite a typical stylist handbook that reflects its authors' assumption "that the qualities of 'good' writing remain essentially the same, no matter what the mode or purpose for writing." Those who are indeed knowledgeable about the process of writing will immediately write off such an assumption. Yet many practices used by writing teachers are based on just such beliefs. It is the concern of Odell, Cooper, and Courts that new and accurate assumptions about the nature of writing be considered by teachers of written composition, and it is to that end that their comments are directed. The writers begin by noting Kinneavy's theory that purpose in discourse is all important. The aim of discourse determines everything else in the process of discourse. If one embraces this theory, then as Kinneavy suggests, the modes of discourse, narration, exposition, description and argument are important only insofar as they enable a writer to accomplish a certain purpose. Another assumption about writing held by current theorists is that one's choices must be guided by a complex awareness of speaker, subject, and audience, not by a single set of conventions. For such writers as James Moffett, Walter Gibson, and Kinneavy, the relation of speaker, subject, and audience is basic to all types of discourse.

Yet the typical stylist handbook hardly treats this relationship and merely notes that a writer should not loose respect for his audience. In this article by Cooper, Odell and Courts, complex questions are raised such as 'How do writers actually go about choosing diction, syntactic and organizational patterns, and content?" Questions about published writing, writing done at different age levels, and about eliciting and assessing writing performance are also raised.

Suppose researchers were to find that, for example, explicit statements about purpose could be omitted from writing assignments without affecting writers' performance on those assignments. If this were the case, one would have to consider the possibility that, at least under some circumstances, purpose in writing might not be as important as we think it is.

> Purpose and meaning determine our outcomes in composition. Never sacrifice your purpose.
>
> — DONDA RULE #42

Implied in this article, and in the above statement in particular, are certain aspects of a systems methodology where one is necessarily obliged to define problems accurately, reassess current practices and apply only those methods that will contribute to effective writing.

James Britton touches on several interesting possibilities regarding the composing process, using a research study involving 500 boys and girls in their first, third, fifth, and seventh years of schooling in 65 schools scattered over England and Wales. Using 2,000 scripts written by the students on a range of subjects, the researchers drew conclusions and established categories that are rarely discussed by those concerned with the writing process. A discussion of contextualization and conceptualization and the composing process is particularly meaningful in the context of systems theory. Britton notes that in some situations writing is conceptualized in a piecemeal fashion. Some parts of discourse readers may ignore because they are too familiar; others they may reject because they judge them, for a variety of reasons to be unacceptable; others may be rejected because they cannot interpret them. Around those fragments readers accept, they will build their own connections, articulating the new information with what was already familiar to them.

Britton argues, however, that readers must resist the process of piecemeal conceptualization, responding to the work as a whole and suspending judgment until the shape of the whole has been reconstructed in the reading. Otherwise, we are in danger of misinterpreting the message as we may locate the message in some detail rather than in the construct as a whole. According to Britton, "The conventions of poetic discourse (and perhaps of all discourse) thus call for global contextualization."

In his discussion on contextualization and the composing process, Britton notes that "writers were likely to succeed if they found for their opening a generalization powerful enough to require more than a sentence or two to work out its implications.

"Planning in advance is no guarantee of success," says Britton, who further states that "an outline does not necessarily promote the coherence that arises in the texture of writing—and indeed may often militate against it." The use of an outline as a way of insuring an orderly and well written essay is itself a piecemeal approach that appears to be ineffective much of the time. As Britton notes in a discussion of preparation, incubation, and articulation, "that thinking and utterance may undergo organizing processes at an involuntary level has been demonstrated often enough."

In *Paradigms and Problems: Needed Research in Rhetorical Invention*, Richard Young asks, "what basis can one argue that we need certain kinds of research in rhetorical invention and that we are less in need of other kinds?" He continues, "I would like to move toward an answer by first proposing that since the beginning of the century, the teaching and researching of composition have been guided by what Thomas Kuhn (1970) has called a 'paradigm,' a system of widely shared values, beliefs, and methods that determines the nature and conduct of the discipline. A paradigm determines what is included in the discipline and what is excluded from it, what is taught and not taught, what problems are regarded as important and unimportant, and, by implication, what research is regarded as valuable in developing the discipline . . . It is not difficult to find evidence for the contrary position that there has been no generally shared system of beliefs which has guided work in the discipline."

Sometimes the big concept of your writing is expressed in a very simple way.

— Donda Rule #43

In this extended quote, Young addresses the essence of this dissertation as he points out the need for a shared conceptual framework for the teaching of writing today. Within his essay, Young notes a number of theories and practices currently held in the discipline of written composition, citing such theorists and rhetoricians as Kenneth Burke, Kenneth Pike, Janet Emig, Wayne C. Sooth, and Edward Corbett. But of most importance is Young's assertion that written composition has no shared system of beliefs to guide work in the area. Noting that there has been some allegiance to past theories and practices in the teaching of writing, Young addresses the issue of classical rhetoric and its relevance to contemporary rhetoric and comments extensively on what has been labeled the current-traditional paradigm for teachers of written composition.

According to Young, "The main difficulty in discussing the current-traditional paradigm, or in even recognizing its existence, is that so much of our theoretical knowledge about it is tacit." Young notes that emphasis has been placed on the composed product rather than the composing process. According to Young, the whole of written composition has been reduced to the classification of discourse into description, exposition, narration, and argument and to an analysis of discourse into words, sentences, and paragraphs.

Further, Young states, "we are confronted with a fundamental educational problem for which current-traditional rhetoric offers no solution." Young believes that the primary goal of a writing class is self-discovery, which implies that composition must be viewed as a process. Indeed the writing teacher must shift from focusing on the composed product and devote more attention to the composition process.

> Your grade on an essay is less important than your self discovery.
>
> — DONDA RULE #44

The latter part of Young's article is devoted to a discussion on needed research. He begins by noting that our discipline appears to be in a crisis state that calls for research quite different from that carried on under the current traditional paradigm.

Young argues, "Research appropriate to the present situation, however, must be directed toward determining the adequacy of the present paradigm and the proposed alternatives." It is a broader perspective that Young advocates. Like the systems theorists, Young points out the necessity for identifying problems accurately and for re-assessing current theories and practices in a discipline where traditional approaches do not appear to meet the needs of either students or teachers.

However, as Young states, "The existence of a persistent problem in the current-traditional paradigm does not itself provide a basis for repudiating it. For no matter how dissatisfied teachers and scholars have been with current traditional rhetoric—and the dissatisfaction has been substantial—they will not renounce the paradigm that has led them into crisis unless there is an acceptable alternative to take its place."

What teachers and researchers must do then, is investigate other possibilities for a conceptual framework that might be shared in the discipline of written composition. Further, such a framework must allow for the many possibilities that have gone virtually unnoticed or with little attention. Invention, for example, a major aspect of classical rhetoric, was set aside until teachers concentrated on more tacit skills, those that could easily be measured. Pre-writing is another vital aspect of the composing process that is only beginning to receive the attention one must give it to teach writing effectively. It is a way of viewing the writing process, and consequently, the world, that writing teachers must adopt to be more effective in the classroom. Further, this view or paradigm must be so comprehensive that it dare not leave out any known aspect of the composing process as all are essential to the development of better writers.

Both experimental research and the development of new theories about the nature and teaching of writing, clearly indicate, as D'Angelo and others have noted, a need for a theory that encompasses all that is known about writing and that is flexible enough for addition, deletion, or alteration as the knowledge about writing changes or increases. Educators have spent a great deal of time arguing about the best theory or the best techniques, while students continue to suffer.

When teachers argue about technique and methods, students suffer.

— DONDA RULE #45

The inconsistency, ignorance, hesitation, and fear that often characterize the individuals who must teach students to write may well stem from the fact that there is at present, no single framework universally accepted by writing instructors that is broad enough to accommodate all the factors involved in teaching writing. Bit by bit, information is discovered and presented about the teaching of written composition, cut except for one or two theories like those of Pike and D'Angelo, little attempt has been made to integrate the useful aspects of existing studies and theories and to develop a conceptual framework for the teaching of written composition. By and large students are still required to complete activities prescribed by the teachers, activities that are often incomplete in themselves addressing some aspects of writing, but ignoring others.

When one considers the many methods and ideas that have been offered by various scholars regarding the teaching of written composition, it is astounding that students still have such enormous difficulty with writing. Composing an essay or even a letter often poses severe problems for a large number of students, many of whom find such activities almost devastating. It appears as though all of the theories and techniques that have come forth about teaching writing have not effected any real change in the writing ability of students. For with all the existing knowledge about writing instruction, something more is needed. Still there remains the need for a unifying framework that is able to address itself to an infinite number of possibilities regarding the teaching of writing. There remains the need for a systems perspective in which interrelationships are examined and understood and where parts considered important in the development of writing skills, whether they involve lengthening of T-units or sentence combining, are viewed in relation to each other and to the whole. Such a perspective, a systems perspective, has gained acceptance in a number of disciplines since its emergence in the field of science. The following chapter attempts to examine the concept of systems as it relates to the nature of writing and to writing instruction, and to suggest that systems thinking in itself may provide for the unifying framework needed 1n the teaching of written composition. Actually, what follows is not another theory or approach that is being suggested, but a way of viewing the total writing process as an encompassing system that allows for a wide range of possibilities for improving the writing performances of secondary school and college students.

6
SYSTEMS PHILOSOPHY AS THE THEORETICAL BASE OF TEACHING WRITTEN COMPOSITION

ACCORDING TO HOWARD PIERSON, "Two attitudes discourage the teaching of writing today. One is that writing is too difficult to teach. The other is that there is no need to learn "how to write." The former attitude is widely held by a number of instructors who have puzzled long hours over how to teach students to write acceptable prose. The latter may be more questionable, in that many teachers still see an urgent need for students to acquire good writing skills.

The attitudes of those who teach writing vary from one extreme to another, and as society moves from in age of certain determinism, and relatively few choices, to one of uncertainty, indeterminism, and a great number of choices, the arguments about the proper methodology for teaching writing increase. Competent writing instructors can no longer insist that students learn traditional grammar as a primary means of improving their writing ability. They must consider many other factors. They must concern themselves with the individual needs of each student realizing that there are many factors that come into play in the process of helping students to improve their writing ability. They must know what methods to use in the classroom, when to use them and why. The choices or methods suggested are increasing daily; however, many students remain unable to write effectively.

They must concern themselves with the individual needs of each student.

— DONDA RULE #46

With the many theories, methods, and research studies advocating methods of teaching written composition, one might wonder why students still have difficulty in composing acceptable prose. One reason may be that teachers of written composition have yet to embrace an underlying philosophy that can serve as a basis for instruction. Consequently, the writing teacher often proceeds from a fragmented and thus limited perspective that disallows the students' acquisition of good writing skills. The work of Hunt, Bateman and Zidonis, and Christensen, among others, and the theories of Chomsky, Pike, or D'Angelo are important, but what may be most helpful to students of written composition, is an understanding that the written composition as well as the process of learning to write is multidimensional, involving a large number of interrelated and interdependent parts.

Composing is interdependent and interdisciplinary.

— DONDA RULE #47

Hence, the need for a paradigm for teachers and students of written composition becomes more and more apparent. Such a paradigm or unifying framework is what Frank D'Angelo refers to as "a conceptual theory of rhetoric," what Young and Becker call "theoretical principles necessary for a distinctly new approach to rhetoric and what Virginia Burke calls "a flexible theory as the informing discipline for the teaching of composition. Where can one turn to find the philosophical base that is presently missing in the discipline of written composition? The systems theory, because it allows for the viewing of phenomena from an integrated perspective, may provide teachers of written composition with the broader perspective that is needed in helping students to improve significantly in writing. The purpose of this chapter is to explore the dynamics of systems philosophy and its implications for the teacher of written composition and to suggest that such a theory might serve as the underlying philosophy needed in the teaching of written composition.

WHAT IS SYSTEMS THEORY? A REVIEW

In chapter one, a detailed description was given of systems theory. This theory involves a way of looking at phenomena in terms of integrated relations rather than in terms of fragmented parts. It takes into account that an interrelationship exists between all elements and constituents of a whole or system and that each essential factor of any system must always be considered and evaluated as interdependent components of a total system. Contrary to this belief it was once widely held that the whole was equal to the sum total of its parts, an additive view that is thought by many today to be inadequate. It is not the mere piecing together of bricks, lumber, nails, cement, and the hundreds of other elements used, but it is the ordering of these materials -- the interrelationships that exist among and between them — that constitute the whole. From its conceptualization to the laying of the final brick, a building or any system is the result of many factors coming together in particular ways to yield the whole. Too, the whole is not irreducible to the sum of its parts. For if any given building should be torn apart by a storm or a blast, and if each of the individual elements or parts were to remain intact on the premises, still they would not yield the building or the whole as the interrelationships would have been destroyed. Parts alone do not constitute the whole, and thus it is essential that an observer understand that any system, any whole results from the dynamic interaction of parts. Such is the nature of systems. In short, a system can be defined as any phenomenon having interrelated parts that function as a complex, mutually dependent, interacting elements, as a part of a larger whole.

Advocates of the systems view hold that the atomistic framework that once dominated the thinking of scholars before the introduction of systems theory, is no longer adequate for viewing phenomena, and that the broader perspective afforded by systems theory is essential in today's educational process. As Wooton states, "If we are to deal effectively with the challenges of today, it seems clear to me that we cannot expect to solve our problems by focusing on them within the perspective of the past." It is my belief that systems analysis or the systems approach can provide some of the answers we need to deal with the weaknesses of our present day system.

Systems Theory: A Philosophy in Teaching Composition

For many years those concerned with helping students to write clear and meaningful prose have sought to find methods to do so. Literally thousands have participated in the struggle to find effective ways to foster good writing, and a wealth of information has been pursued from a fragmented perspective as individual factors affecting the writing ability of students have been examined but have not been considered in light of a total process as interrelated parts of a whole. For example, if the writing teacher views sentence combining as an effective tool in writing instruction, yet fails to understand it as a part of an entire network and fails to introduce it at the proper time and to those students who are likely to benefit from it, an exposure to sentence combining is not likely to yield many positive results.

> Writing teachers must know when to implement components. If lesson plans lack meaning and proper timing, entire unit plans can be void of function and learning.
>
> — Donda Rule #48

Further, sentence combining is but one exercise that appears to be of some use to some students at some particular stage in the students' pursuit of better writing skills. There are probably hundreds of other factors that may come into play when a student attempts a written exercise. The systems view provides a way of looking at these factors as autonomous wholes and as dependent parts that are necessary in teaching writing. It is not just the factors in isolation that must concern writing teachers. They must regard as essential the identification of the important factors both in the teaching of written composition and the writing process. They must understand the interrelationships that exist between them.

Laszlo proclaims, "The ideal of rigorous information, while it atomized our understanding, did give us a healthy respect for tested knowledge. We are no longer willing to put up with theories that stitch together gaps in knowledge with the fabric of pure faith or imagination. But those who believe that such a patchwork approach is the only means of gaining a coherent and integrated world view are mistaken."

D'Angelo says, "Any new rhetoric should take into account larger views. Any new rhetoric should focus on logical and nonlogical modes of thought, on reason and imagination, on thinking and feeling, on linearity and holism, on personal writing as well as on expository and persuasive writing . . . Rhetoric should be not just of the age of technology, but of the Cosmic Age."

Essentially, D'Angelo suggests that any new rhetoric should reflect a new and broader consciousness. "There is no magic formula for producing a theory of discourse, or for that matter, for generating any kind of scientific theory. The theorist begins by noticing the lack of explanatory principles in a particular field or the unsatisfactory nature of existing principles in that field. It is usually a field in which at least some facts, some ideas, some regularities, some generalizations, however crude they may be, have already been established. But the theorist feels a need to bring all of these detached, separate facts and generalizations into a coherent framework. So he looks about for a conceptual scheme, a working hypothesis, a controlling metaphor to explain facts that previously appeared to be unrelated."

The writing teacher, like the scientist, must now be concerned with more than accumulating remarkably detailed but detached facts about the teaching of written composition. If one agrees with D'Angelo that the composition is an organic development, and that one of the main tasks of any new rhetoric is to describe fully, precisely, and clearly, the syntactical relationships that extend beyond the limits of the sentence and paragraph, and to describe equally as fully the meaning or conceptual relationships in writing, then the writing instructor must cease to concentrate on detail only without regard for the wider structure that gives it context.

> Students should focus on context before detail. If context is studied and embraced, the details will surface due to the context.
>
> — Donda Rule #49

The writing instructor, like the new scientist must "concentrate on structure on all levels of magnitude and complexity and must fit detail into its general framework. Instructors must discern relationships and situations, not atomistic facts and events.

The concept of systems provided by the contemporary sciences may equip the writing instructor with a theoretical base, a new way of ordering the information we already have and are likely to get in the foreseeable future. General systems theory may enable writing instructors to be of greater help to their students.

Systems Theory, Research Studies, and Writing Methods

In recent years much effort has gone into finding effective ways to teach written composition. Classroom teachers, theorists, graduate students, and many others concerned about the inability of so many students to write effectively have embarked on what appears to be an almost desperate search for effective teaching methods. Thus, a number of research studies, theories, and methods have been forthcoming. However, as pointed out in chapter one, Floyd Matson notes that to view an object in isolation without consideration for its relationship to a larger environment, often results in misinformation.

Roy Grinker notes that parts are understood in light of the whole. Laszlo points out that one trouble with the specialist is that he concentrates on detail without regard for the larger structure. All three of these observations can be applied to most of the research conducted in written composition. Kellogg Hunt, for example, examines very thoroughly a wide range of grammatical structures that exist in student writing. Although Hunt assumed that quality of writing "improves" with chronological age, he did not deal directly with the problem of holistic evaluation of student writing. Morenberg, Daiker, and Kerek addressed the relationship between T-unit length and overall quality. In addition to quantity, the quality of writing should also be considered if the total picture of writing is to be assessed most accurately. Questions such as these must be considered even when the focus of the study is on such factors as grammatical structure. A researcher cannot be expected to examine a large number of aspects of writing in an individual study. But the researcher can be expected to conduct the study from an integrated perspective, thus exhibiting an awareness of the whole in the explanation of one particular part.

J.P. Bockart notes that many educators blindly focus on one particular method of instruction at a time, becoming so engrossed in the one method that others are not considered. Hunt focused on structural aspects of writing and appeared to be concerned almost solely with the final quantitative product. However, to produce effective writing involves more than the lengthening of sentences. Effective writing involves a number of factors, many of that are rarely considered in the current research. D'Angelo says new approaches emphasize feeling rather than intellect, exploration and discovery rather than preconceived ideas, the imagination, creativity, free association, fantasy, play, dreams, the unconscious, non intellectual sensing the stream of consciousness, and the self.

> Beware of long sentences and quantity. If meaning and purpose are sacrificed in a long sentence, make it shorter and clear.
> — DONDA'S RULE #50

Here D'Angelo presents essential aspects of writing that Hunt does not address, aspects that are important in the development of a methodology for teaching writing. To the student who has begun to formulate ideas and seeks a more mature way of expressing them, the methods suggested by the Hunt study may be useful. But the study in isolation, may be of little, if any benefit. For no matter how thorough a researcher may be, his study is part of a wider structure, a larger system. Like the finger of the human hand, it serves little purpose detached, apart from the total system. And if the study itself fosters the tendency on the part of writing instructors to focus only on a particular detail or activity without regard for the broader context, fragmentation occurs, usually paralleled by very little growth in the writing ability of students. One cannot deny that students may benefit from a knowledge of grammatical structures, and few would deny that a sentence building program may aid students in improving their writing. But these aspects should be presented to the students as only part of the ongoing process of writing, as interrelated and interdependent parts of the whole.

Although Bateman and Zidonis were concerned as was Hunt, with structural aspects of the sentence, the sentence evaluation techniques used in their study appear to reflect a broader perspective. Not only were the researchers concerned about the grammatical or structural richness of the sentence, but with the "proportion of well-formed sentences and the trend in the frequency and kinds of grammatical misoperations that occur in pupil writing as well." Unlike the structural linguist, Bateman and Zidonis show concern for the well-framed sentence as a grammatical goal, realizing that the mere stringing together of words does not necessarily result in clear and meaningful sentences. Like the systems scholar, Bateman and Zidonis investigated deeper levels of grammatical constructions through the use of transformational grammar rather than traditional or structural. Realizing that the thinking processes cannot be overlooked in the process of creating a sentence, Bateman and Zidonis were concerned that the students not merely produce sentences, but understand structurally the involvement in generating a well-formed sentence. Bateman and Zidonis also indicate an awareness of the fact that meaning (thinking) and structure are inextricably bound and to consider one without regard for the other would be a fragmented approach.

Although Bateman and Zidonis reveal their belief that creative thinking is an important aspect of writing, they are not directly concerned with this aspect in their study; thus they present a limited perspective. For no grammar alone will probably be able to provide for today's students the stimulus needed to encourage creative thinking. And as Douglas Alley states about the kind of theory needed for the teaching of rhetoric, it must not be content with the importation of Latin terminology or the manipulation of language patterns (though both of these devices may be of some benefit to the student), but must base its subject matter and its practices on the processes of all types of thinking [and] especially that of creative thinking.

Because each aspect of writing, structural or otherwise, is an interrelated and interdependent part of the wholes, a thorough understanding of any one aspect seems to necessitate some understanding of all aspects. The instructor who appreciates the importance of structure, for example, but fails to consider the importance of such aspects as motivation, may cause some students to become more inhibited about writing. Until the student has formulated ideas and is somewhat confident about articulating them, methods concerning structural aspects will be of little use to both teacher and student.

> Students must be confident in formulating ideas. If not, their writing will suffer.
>
> — DONDA RULE #51

No matter how complete a research study appears, it is still lacking if it does not reflect the new and broader consciousness that good writing does not result from mechanistic and rigidly prescribed activities. Good writing results from the ordering of many aspects that are themselves both autonomous holons and interdependent parts. Martin notes that in many instances in education, knowledge is not integrated. While some research studies may help one to see more clearly some of the techniques needed in the teaching of written composition, unless placed in proper perspective, they can and probably will be misleading.

In most studies, phenomena is viewed in relative isolation without regard for the whole. An outdated framework for the teaching of writing is reflected as bits of information are gained but not integrated as interdependent parts of a larger whole.

The researcher in most instances has not viewed the teaching of writing from an integrated perspective recognizing the importance or a multitude of factors. It appears that each attaches himself to one or two aspects that may affect writing ability and begins a thorough exploration of those aspects alone. Such practices tend to have little impact on students of written composition and according to John Michaelis. "Research has done little to suggest new practices to replace the old." A number of rhetoricians, some of whose theories reflect an awareness of systems theory, agree that a new and more encompassing theory is needed in the teaching of writing. Unlike most of the empirical research conducted in written composition, some of the theories reflect an awareness that the essay results from the dynamic interaction of parts. Roger Sale, for example, comments extensively on several aspects of writing, but his major thesis is that writing can be learned but it cannot be taught.

Writing is not a teachable series of actions or patterns . . . What teachers can do is to ask questions, to praise and to criticize, to offer alternate ways of thinking about things. They get someone started, or help him along, in a process of his making himself to be careful about himself and the way he thinks and speaks and writes.

Essentially, Sale believes that learning should not be prescribed by the teacher, but merely facilitated. His obvious concern about student-centered curricula reflects what one systems scholar regards as essential in using a systems approach. Randall, like Sale, believes that the broadest perspective must be learner-centered. Writing is a process that involves the students' experiences and the students' own ability to think creatively determines to a large degree the extent to which they will be able to master the skill of writing. Clearly Sale's point of view is crucial in the teaching of writing, allowing the writing instructor to view a number of different and interacting factors involved in the writing process and to note as a whole the progress of the student. Both instructor and students are then free to work from an integrated rather than fragmented perspective. The philosophy of Hans Guth is similar to that of Sale's in that he too believes that personal experiences and thinking abilities of students are extremely important aspects of writing. Guth is concerned with both form and content and notes that one is needed to facilitate the other. In the words of Guth,

"Principles of organization and of style cannot be taught in the abstract, to be applied to such materials as may come along. They must be taught to the student as a means of giving structure and form to what he knows and thinks and feels. The student must come to regard rhetoric not as the art of putting pre-conceived opinions into words but of discovering and shaping what he has to say. Learning to write cannot be separated from learning to observe and to think."

Too often, writing instructors attempt to do just what Guth argues against. They fragment the teaching of form and content, treating each as separate detached elements of writing. Such fragmented activities may stem from earlier approaches that held that a knowledge of traditional grammar, for example, would facilitate good writing. Many continue to focus on detail, without regard for the broader context. Structure and meaning are interrelated like all elements of good writing. When singled out to be studied as individual aspects of writing, each should be studied with full knowledge of the other.

> Structure and meaning are interrelated like all elements of good writing.
>
> — DONDA RULE #52

Edward P. J. Corbett points out the value of classical rhetoric in teaching students in today's classrooms to write more effectively.

Although the use of classical rhetoric in a modern theory has received some criticism from rhetoricians such as Pike, Young, Becker, and Booth, Corbett maintains,

"Classical rhetoric . . . in the main, offers positive advice to help students in composition of a specific kind of discourse directed to a definite audience for a particular purpose."

Even though the modern theories seem to offer more possibilities for the student who is just learning to write, some aspects of classical rhetoric, the six divisions of discourse, for example, may at some point be helpful to the beginning writer. It may provide the organizational structure needed by the writer to express his thoughts clearly. But, again, the divisions of classical rhetoric represent a vehicle for expressing thought and should be used as a tool to do so, not as an exercise that may even inhibit growth. D'Angelo and Corbett see merit in the revival of classical rhetoric, believing that a new theory should combine the old and the new. D'Angelo is more concerned that a new theory reflect an awareness of new discoveries and that these discoveries be taken into account in describing the writing process. D'Angelo discusses the argument of the imagination versus the rational by forwarding the process of composing is often thought to be so intuitive and mysterious that any attempt to plumb its mysteries is looked on with disfavor. According to some critics, the process of composition originates in the imagination, and the imagination is not accessible to observation. Other critics believe that the process of composition originates in the rational processes of the mind. As we have seen, both of these views are partial: that the mind has two major modes of consciousness, the rational and the intuitive, and that these modes may operate simultaneously in the normal individual.

D'Angelo's conceptual theory of rhetoric addresses such problems as the relationship between thought and structure, the former stemming primarily from the imaginative process and the latter, from the rational.

> Let knowledge and imagination lead the writing process.
>
> — DONDA RULE #53

The interrelationships of parts is extremely important in D'Angelo's theory, but he notes, as do other advocates of systems philosophy, "the overall shape of discourse is relatively more important than its parts. Without question, D'Angelo's beliefs are congruent with those of the systems scholar. He treats thoroughly both the structural and meaning concepts and approaches the teaching of writing from a scientific perspective. His involvement with the functions of the mind and its relationship to writing represents a paradigmatic shift that is comparable to those made in science and discussed in chapter one.

D'Angelo's ideas are revolutionary, and they represent a distinct break from older theories that have contributed very little to the teaching of writing. In this conceptual theory of rhetoric, traditional sentence diagramming, for example, gives way to an investigation of inter-sentence relationships as D'Angelo studies specific ways in which sentences are interrelated. His theory offers new possibilities in the teaching of writing. D'Angelo insists that "writing should not be the imposing of form on content but rather the adapting of form to the expression." D'Angelo presents writing as a process involving a multitude of factors that must each be examined in view of interrelationships that exist within the essay and in view of each factor's relationship to the essay as a whole.

James Sledd expresses commitment to the linguistic approach to the teaching of writing and points out the inadequacy of traditional approaches. According to Sledd,

"The teacher who knows some linguistics sees the composition course in light of his knowledge; and if he does not foolishly conclude that linguistics is a panacea, his introduction to linguistic science may be part of a general reorientation which is more valuable than any one specific use of linguistics or methods or materials."

It appears that a great number of English teachers should undergo a kind of reorientation in order to eliminate totally those assumptions about the teaching of writing that have proved ineffective and to gain the broader perspective needed for the adoption of new and more effective approaches. Often, an instructor may be unable to abandon ineffective approaches because of an inability to abandon a narrow perspective.

> Most teachers are sheep being led to the slaughterhouse of rote memory, standardized test pressure, inadequate lesson plans, sentence analysis, textbook adoption bullying, central office demands, time constraints, grading nightmares, and social promotion. Don't be a sheep.
>
> — Donda Rule #54

Laszlo comments on the unwillingness of the scientist to give up the old and atomistic framework for the broader world view of systems. But the competent teacher of composition must not cling to old views at the sacrifice of new possibilities in teaching writing. Without an understanding of the nature of language, one that involves more than the prescription of rules, the teacher of writing may become nothing more than a teacher of detached bits of information that have little to do with the actual composing process. Because linguistics requires that language be viewed from a broad perspective, the teacher who approaches the teaching of writing from a linguistic perspective has a wider range of possibilities and will not insist that students be strictly governed by prescribed rules that are in some cases obsolete, and in others detrimental to student achievement. These rigid rules may negate the possibility of real growth on the part of students.

The particle, wave, field theory (only one aspect of tagmemics) enables a teacher or student to view elements of a composition as both wholes and as parts of a larger whole. The trimodal way of viewing a sentence, for example, would involve three different descriptions of the sentence. A particle description emphasizes those features that make it distinctive from other sentences. It is viewed as a whole. A wave description emphasizes the absence of distinct boundaries between sentences even though the sentence still has dynamic features of its own. A field description involves viewing the sentence as nonexistent in its own right.

It cannot be isolated and independent. Rather, the relationships that exist among all the sentences to form the whole essay is what is concentrated upon. The trimodal perspective in describing a sentence is compatible with systems thinking in that the interdependent nature of individual elements and the relationships of parts and wholes is considered. This kind of perspective is needed in teaching students to write. More rhetoricians have begun to note the importance of viewing the essay as a whole comprised of interdependent parts. It is the relationships of many factors that must be considered in understanding thoroughly the nature of writing and the theory presented by Young and Pike is one that not only allows for, but requires that relationships be investigated. Even though such theorists as Roger Sale, Hans Guth, and Frank D'Angelo call for a broader perspective in the teaching of written composition, other theorists, deal primarily with the structural aspects of writing.

In an extended quote by Douglas Alley makes apparent the lack of and need for a theory that deals primarily with the thinking aspect of writing. Alley comments,

> One readily apparent deficiency is the lack of the one basic point of reference on which any rhetoric must be founded. This foundation is not the subject matter of rhetoric, not the analysis of rhetorical products, not the study of the history of rhetoric, and not the prescriptive directions for the formulations of paragraphs or compositions. It is the process one goes through in gaining ideas, and formulating these ideas into a distinctive and significant piece of prose. While the rhetorical product may be of importance to the rhetorician or the artist, the process as a learning experience is of crucial importance to the student, especially the student in the secondary school, whose product is the culmination of this process. Too often teachers are too interested in the product, and because of this, processes of thinking which lead to the product are given little consideration.

As Alley notes, since thinking is the foundation for writing, little can be accomplished in teaching writing if this aspect is ignored or lightly regarded. The teacher of written composition must engage students in activities that will help them in the development of critical and creative thinking. Because structural aspects of writing are easier to observe and to measure, few have attempted to investigate thoroughly the thinking aspect of writing. Laszlo notes, however, that any attempt to observe a particle knocks it off course and makes it different from what it is in reality or in context. When a particle is singled out to be measured, it is no longer the same as it was as an integral part of a larger whole. Again, a finger of the human hand is not the same finger detached from the hand. Alone, it has little if any function. Systems thinking holds that parts are mutually dependent. Thus, it is crucial that the writing instructor identify and effectively deal with those essential aspects such as creative thinking. In fact, any theory, and especially a comprehensive and effective one, should mirror a genuine concern for the thinking aspect of written composition since it is as crucial as any factor in producing effective prose. But even greater, a theory for teaching writing should reflect an awareness that not form, not content, or any single aspect can be regarded lightly. For all are parts of a larger and more important whole.

> The process leads to the complete composition.
>
> — DONDA RULE #55

THE WRITTEN COMPOSITION PROCESS AS A SYSTEM

Repeatedly, a system has been defined as a complex whole resulting from the interaction of interrelated and mutually dependent parts. Any phenomenon might be viewed as a system, including that of the written composition, for there are a number of parts that interact in particular ways within the composition itself and constitute the whole. There are also those parts that affect one's desire and ability to write, parts that constitute what might be called a system of writing instruction. The former entails such factors as the actual words, sentences, and paragraphs that comprise the written paper. The latter involves such factors as motivation and methods of teaching that constitute the whole of learning to write. These known and interdependent factors are already large in number, and are increasing rapidly as we learn more about writing as a total process and become more sensitive to the needs of each individual we teach.

Essentially, the process of learning to write and the written composition are both systems having a number of parts that the effective writing instructor must identify and put into proper perspective. The composition itself involves a large number of factors, and because there are so many parts there are a number of ways to approach a discussion of the written composition as a system. Generally, however, one may view the composition in much the same way one might view a building or any other system.

There are so many factors or parts that interact to yield the written composition that an attempt to describe all interrelationships that exist within the composition would be futile. But to illustrate further the interrelatedness of parts of an essay, one might note the relationship of a sentence to a paragraph of which it is a part. Consider this sentence extracted from a paragraph in Paulo Friere's *Pedagogy of the Oppressed*. The sentence reads: "One of the basic elements of the relationship between oppressor and oppressed is that of prescription." This sentence has some meaning within itself. It contains all the elements in correct order so that on one level the reader understands the point being expressed by the writer. It is different from the other sentences in the paragraph and stands alone as a whole unto itself. On the other hand, the sentence is also a dependent part, depending on other sentences, the paragraph, and the writing in its entirety to provide an even clearer picture of what the writer is saying. Thus, the sentence is part of a larger process, a constituent of the paragraph of which it is a part.

Consider the sentence in the context of the total paragraph:

The "fear of freedom" which afflicts the oppressed, a fear which may equally well lead them to desire the role of oppressor or bind them to the role of oppressed, should be examined. One of the basic elements of the relationship between oppressor and oppressed is 'prescription.' Every prescription represents the imposition of one individual's choice upon another, transforming the consciousness of the person prescribed to into one that conforms with the prescriber's consciousness. Thus, the behavior of the oppressed is a prescribed behavior, following as it does the guidelines of the oppressor.

Upon reading the paragraph in its entirety, or even after reading the first sentence of the paragraph, one is able to see the continuity that exists between sentences. A melding of sorts. In the first sentence the writer makes known his opinion that the "fear of freedom" should be examined. In the second sentence, he proceeds to begin such an examination by noting the presence of prescription in the relationship between oppressor and oppressed. The third sentence gives the second sentence even more clarity in that the reader learns more about the nature of prescription. Finally, in the last sentence, the writer synthesizes the points previously made in the paragraph and concludes that the behavior of the oppressed is prescribed. In this one paragraph alone, constituted by the interaction of 488 letters, 93 words, five commas, four periods, two apostrophes, one set of quotation marks, reflective and critical thought, and perhaps other underlying factors such as the writer's motivation, there are many interrelationships that one might explore.

Viewing the paragraph as a process involving the interaction of many mutually dependent parts, one is able to see in this writing the hierarchical structure that characterizes any system. As Koestler notes, however, hierarchic organization is not used in reference to order of rank or a linear scale or ladder, but to describe the organization of any system and to suggest that systems are multi-leveled and should be thought of as such. The hierarchic structure of the paragraph is explained by Koestler as follows:

"Its correct symbol is not a rigid ladder but a living tree — a multi-leveled, stratified, out-branching into sub-systems, which branch into sub-systems of lower order, and so on; a structure encapsulating sub-structures and so on; a process of activating sub-processes and so on."

Clearly the paragraph written by Friere (or any other well-written piece of prose) is characterized by hierarchic structure as paragraphs (systems), branching into sentences (subsystems), which branch into words (subsystems of a lower order) and so on.

Koestler's comments regarding parts and wholes of a system might also be applied to the well written piece of prose. He notes:

"A part; as we generally use the word, means something fragmentary and incomplete, which by itself would have no legitimate existence. On the other hand, there is a tendency among the holists to use the other word "whole" or "Gestalt" as something complete in itself which needs no further explanation. But wholes and parts in this absolute sense do not exist anywhere . . . What we find are intermediary structures on a series of levels in ascending order of complexity, each of which has two faces looking in opposite directions: the face turned toward the lower level is that of an autonomous whole, the one turned upward that of a dependent part."

While one may view any given sentence as an autonomous holon with meaning in and of itself, in looking at the broader context of the paragraph, one recognizes that the complete meaning cannot be understood fully in isolation from the rest of the paragraph or total composition. As Daniel Lerner notes, parts do not possess characteristics independently of one another.

Moreover, parts are so closely related that an alteration in one of them causes a change in all of them. Thus, if in the second sentence Friere had used another word instead of "prescription," the use of the word "prescription" in subsequent sentences would not have the same effect because the conscious repetition of the word in some form helps to provide continuity within the paragraph. The word is part of a whole, and in being part, is dependent on the whole to be most meaningful.

> Don't diminish the part for the whole; don't diminish the whole for the part. They need one another.
>
> — DONDA RULE #56

Learner also pointed out that the functional whole could not be properly analyzed from an additive point of view. Thus letters, words, sentences, and all constituents of a piece of writing cannot be piled together to yield the whole. Likewise, a whole is not reducible to the sum of its parts. For like the building, a written composition cannot be dismantled part by part and remain cohesive. For when parts are extracted they differ significantly from what they were in context of the whole. Like the fingers of the human hand, they are more functional as interrelated and interdependent parts of the total essay.

Clearly the written composition is a system, and clearly the parts that interact to constitute the system are numerous. Understanding the written composition as a system is not a difficult task. For years, writing instructors have known that a number of parts interact to yield the completed product. Nevertheless, little attempt has been made to investigate interrelationships and the bits-and-pieces approach continues to dominate the field of writing instruction. As Laszlo notes, we are just beginning to realize the need for connecting probes with one another and gaining some coherent insight into what is there.

An understanding of the written composition as a system is vitally important to the writing instructor. Equally, as important however, is an understanding of the process of teaching writing as a system. For writing instruction involves many interrelated and interdependent parts that yield effective teaching only when used in proper perspective. The known factors that positively affect the writing ability of students must be manipulated by the writing instructor in particular ways to inspire good writing. These factors, which include the theories, strategies, and activities used by the writing instructor, must be examined for their effectiveness in aiding each individual to improve writing skills. The rhetoric of Francis Christensen, for example, is useful in the system of writing instruction, especially in terms of being a powerful heuristic tool for encouraging students to think logically and creatively. However, some students may become even more inhibited about writing if such activities as sentence combining are prescribed without regard for the particular need of the individual student.

Essentially, the instructors' approach to teaching of written composition from a systems perspective will be open to a wide range of possibilities in their teaching. They will not hesitate to draw upon many resources, designing activities to fit the needs of students and applying them at the appropriate time in order to aid in the personal growth of the students. They will realize that the system of writing instruction is limited not to the theories of Hunt, Christensen, and others, but only insomuch as the imagination and creativity of the instructor. There may be several strategies the writing instructor might use during the course of one year or several years. These approaches must not be piecemeal and shortsighted, but should reflect an awareness that there are many factors which come into play in teaching students to write. No factor or part is any less important to the whole than any other factor and any approach adequate for the teaching of writing must necessarily reflect this point of view.

> Students should write daily, regardless of school subject. The practice of writing should be habitual.
>
> — DONDA RULE #57

In terms of a systems philosophy, writing should be viewed as a process that involves a multitude of factors both known and unknown.

These factors must be thought of not as separate, detached, and independent parts joined together to produce an essay, but as interdependent and interrelated parts that work systematically, to produce the more important whole. Each factor should be considered separately so that the depth that is needed for a thorough understanding is not sacrificed, but there must always be the awareness that individual parts must be considered in light of the total essay. Writing should be thought of as a process that involves or reflects life, and thus the writer's personal experiences both in and out of the classroom must be seriously regarded and broadened to achieve the desired results.

Writing should be thought of as a creative process that involves the use of structure to express ideas. Activities should enhance the student's ability to structure thought more clearly. However, structure should not be imposed on thinking, but used only as a vehicle to express thoughts. Writing should be regarded as an activity that necessitates critical thinking, an aspect that is fundamental to all good writing. The rhetorical product is not an end in itself, but a means to greater ends, a way to develop and express ideas that contribute in some fashion to the whole of life.

> Writing should be regarded as an activity that necessitates critical thinking, an aspect that is fundamental to all good writing.
>
> — DONDA RULE #58

In other words, writing should be a learning experience, a liberating experience, a process that aids in the personal development of each writer. It should serve a purpose for the writer beyond that of satisfying a course requirement.

Finally, writing should be viewed as a system that involves various relationships within the written composition as well as outside factors that affect one's ability and desire to write. It is only when writing is considered a process that involves many interdependent factors (a system) that one is able to really understand and appreciate it fully and teach it successfully.

Several systems approaches have been offered by various scholars as models for applying systems philosophy to educational practice. While some still appear to be mechanistic in nature, consisting essentially of flowcharts, graphs, and sometimes prescribed behavioral objectives, other models are open-ended allowing the teacher of written composition the flexibility needed in today's diverse classrooms, while providing the general structure needed to approach the teaching of writing concretely. John Hayman presents a systems approach or a methodology based on the concept of systems that might well serve as a model in the teaching of written composition.

The following chapter is an attempt to suggest specific ways in which the teacher of written composition might apply the systems theory, utilizing the approach outlined by John Hayman. Such an approach clearly reflects a broader consciousness and may aid the writing instructor in facilitating growth in the writing ability of students.

7

IMPLEMENTING A SYSTEMS APPROACH IN THE TEACHING OF WRITTEN COMPOSITION

THE PREVIOUS CHAPTERS have been devoted primarily to a discussion of systems philosophy and its utilization in education and more specifically in the teaching of written composition. Such a philosophy, that of systems theory, has been advocated for decades in various fields of study perhaps because of its encompassing nature. A number of approaches to education have been developed based on systems theory. Some of these approaches have only reinforced the mechanistic and dehumanizing aspects of present-day education, but others have enabled educators to facilitate the growth of their students.

The purpose of this chapter is to suggest how this systems approach might be utilized in the teaching of written composition, an approach that is integrated rather than fragmented and broad enough to encompass the new and broader consciousness called for by contemporary rhetoricians. The discussion that follows will involve the explanation of each step as it applies to the teaching of written composition. Practical suggestions for the writing instructor will be offered also.

> Identify the problems before trying to answer questions.
>
> — DONDA RULE #59

— DONDA RULE #59

The first step in implementing a systems approach is to identify the problem. This step may appear obvious, but as R. A. Kaufman points out, "people will select, produce, and implement solutions before the problem has been identified and substantiated." For many writing instructors, the problem seems apparent and can be summed up by Robert McElroy.

> If your children are attending college, they probably won't be able to write ordinary, expository English with any real degree of structure and lucidity. If they are in high school and planning to attend college, they will write English at the minimal college level when they get there. If they are not planning to attend college, their skills in writing English may not even qualify them for work that a 6th grader can accomplish. And if they are attending elementary school, they are almost certainly not being given the kind of required reading material, much less writing instruction, that might make it possible for them eventually to write comprehensible English.

Quite simply, McElroy points out that students enrolled in schools today are not learning to write. Often the problem is identified but large numbers of students aren't trained or required to write acceptable prose. However, to insure thoroughness in defining the problem, an instructor should consider underlying factors that may influence students' ability to write. A number of reasons have been given for students' low achievement in writing, ranging from "inadequate grounding in the basics of syntax, structure, and style to popularity of secondary school curricula that no longer require the wide range of reading a student must have if he is to learn to write clearly."

Writing requires reading. Writer's block occurs when students haven't read enough to draw from an adequate literature base.

— DONDA RULE #60

However, for many students the problem is more complex and requires a more thorough investigation on the part of the writing instructor. From an early age and for many reasons, including those induced by poor or unknowledgeable instructors, students become disillusioned with writing. For the most part, writing has represented defeat to them, and often they have seen no functional value in and have demonstrated very little appreciation for written communication. They enter the classroom with little interest, desire or competence in writing, and too often they leave the same way. If problems underlying the more apparent problem are not identified, the system that is developed for teaching students may be inappropriate and virtually ineffective. The teacher who wishes to be thorough in identifying the problem should consider some basic truths about educational practices that appear to foster the teaching of written composition. It may be that one major problem is not that the students are unable to write but that they have no motivation or desire to write. They have not been made to understand the value of writing as a means of developing self.

Writing should be taught as a way to develop self.

— Donda Rule #61

The tendency in education has been to speak only superficially of self-development. Paulo Friere refers to such practices as the banking concept of education noting,

> Education becomes an act of depositing, in which the students are depositories, and the teacher is the depositor. Instead of communicating, the teacher issues communiques and makes deposits that the students patiently receive, memorize, and repeat.

Friere continues, noting that while students have the opportunity to become collectors and cataloguers of the things they store, it is they themselves who become filed away through the lack of creativity, transformation, and knowledge in this misguided system. This is what the teacher of written composition must consider identifying the problem. And in many cases much of the problem might stem from the following terrible modes of instruction.

The teacher teaches and the students are taught; the teacher knows everything and the students know nothing; the teacher thinks and the students are thought about; the teacher talks and the students listen meekly; the teacher disciplines and the students are disciplined; the teacher chooses and enforces his choice, and the students comply; the teacher acts and the students have the illusion of acting through the action of the teacher; the teacher chooses the program content, and the students (who were not consulted) adapt to it.

Admittedly, there are teachers of written composition who have transcended some of the practices mentioned above. But in many instances, the above description (or some parts of it) characterize writing instructors today. And rather than identifying the problem correctly they become part of it.

Teachers of written composition who truly want to aid in the development of students must eliminate these underlying problems and concern themselves with every imaginable factor that may hinder students in their pursuit of better writing skills.

There are several ways in which the writing instructor might go about implementing the first step of the systems approach, that of identifying the problem. Here, two are described. First, the writing instructor may involve the class in a general discussion on the teaching of writing in schools. It is important that a climate be established in which students feel comfortable in responding honestly and candidly without fear of repercussion. This, of course, depends largely on the personality and attitude of instructors who might encourage honest responses from students by being honest themselves. Both teachers and students may approach the discussion as a process of discovery about the process of learning to write within the context of formal education, pointing out both strengths and weaknesses of the present system.

Although the discussion should be broad enough to encompass any question that may arise regarding the subject, the teacher may find benefit in focusing specifically on these questions:

1. What is your attitude toward writing?
2. What do you like most about writing?
3. What do you like least about writing?
4. Do you believe that writing is a valuable skill in a "multimedia" society?
5. Do you often have the desire to express yourself through writing?
6. Have you identified specifically any of the problems you have in writing? What are they?
7. What suggestions might you have for the writing instructor?

These questions can form the basis for an interesting and informative discussion that would benefit both students and teachers in identifying problems. Through such a discussion, the instructor becomes more acutely aware of and more sensitive to the concerns of the students and the students become more aware of the instructors concerns. They are both able to proceed with a clearer understanding and with a more accurate description of the problem, and thus, they become better able to find effective solutions.

In order to identify further the problems of individual students, whether they involve students' inability to think critically or to punctuate correctly, many teachers of writing find it helpful to assign a short paper. This assignment however, should be based on some activity that evokes in students the desire to make a comment. While it is sometimes difficult to find a topic that will appeal to every student, some topics appear to stimulate more interest than others.

> Short writing assignments with provocative prompts should be given.
>
> — DONDA RULE #62

General questions may be raised that inspire students to create topics of their own. One general subject that may evoke a good response is that of education. The teacher may begin a discussion by noting that education is a commodity that often many students are willing to pay for and not receive. The teacher may point out that if any member of the class were to purchase an automobile for instance, they would be quite upset to find that the car was not available at the expected time of delivery. On the other hand, if a teacher misses class on a given day, or sometimes for several days, a considerable percentage of the class rejoices ready to celebrate the unexpected holiday even though tuition has been paid. This observation may serve as a catalyst for a stimulating discussion about education. Both teacher and students begin to question whether or not a formal education is really beneficial to students in developing their own individual selves. Students might be asked to consider such issues as what education means to them, whether or not they are being educated and for what purposes. They will reply in various ways, some expressing the belief that formal education is a worthwhile venture through which one genuinely becomes more knowledgeable. Others may feel that education is not a process of learning at all, but merely a necessary ticket for attaining a particular status in society. Many may never have given much real consideration to the question of education. Nonetheless, it is this kind of inquiry that is particularly vital in the writing class, most likely to stimulate students in the way necessary to produce good writing.

Following the discussion, the teacher should ask the class to write a short paper, one to two pages, to be turned in the next class session. They may specify such topics as: "Is a Formal Education Really Educational?," "Education: A Liberating or Enslaving Experience," and "Education: The Key to Successful Living." Or students may create their own topics based on the class discussion. From the papers, the instructor is able to note specific strengths and weaknesses in the writing ability of each student and may record such findings on an index card to be referred to as the need arises. These two activities, the class discussion on the teaching of writing and the paper on education (or some other stimulating topic), can help to ensure a more accurate and thorough identification of the problem — the first step toward aiding students in becoming effective writers.

The second step in implementing a systems approach is a three part systems analysis process. The instructor must look at the current system, its parts and interrelationships, conduct a needs assessment, and define constraints. In looking at the present system of writing instruction, the teacher will find a large number of methods and theories for teaching writing.

A general review of current practices in the teaching of written composition was presented in chapter five. While many of the approaches suggested may prove useful to students, in and of themselves these approaches may be incomplete. As parts, they are as complete as any part might be. But as Koestler notes, "Wholes and parts in an absolute sense do not exist anywhere. . . . It is a part of a large structure, one in which there are interrelationships among parts, that the methodologies suggested by various rhetoricians can be applied most effectively."

Until recently, there was little attempt on the part of writing instructors to integrate the methods and theories suggested in the teaching of composition. Fragmented approaches prevailed. William H. Evans and Jerry Walker suggest that for many years written composition was taught as an atomistic process, one of mastering separate skills in isolation and gradually putting them together to produce a composition, as if the whole were not more than the sum of its parts. Even having something to say was treated as a skill that could be learned by breaking a topic down into its component parts as in an outline.

The teacher itemized composition skills and arranged them in a learning sequence based on their complexity as determined by the number and order of lexical or syntactic units involved. In the typical sequence, a student learned to spell, to capitalize, and to organize words, first in simple sentences and then in complex, compound, and complex-compound sentences. Then, as he learned to string words together to produce grammatical sentences, he also learned to string sentences together to produce paragraphs, and paragraphs to produce longer compositions. The ability to identify parts preceded the ability to use them.

Such instructional practices clearly reflect the need for an integrated theory as well as an approach for its implementation. Evans and Walker present that few people were satisfied with the products of such a system. Rhetoric instructors in college complained that many of the students being sent to them from high school could write neither "correct" nor interesting prose, their most common complaint being that most of the writing they received was sterile. Employers of students who didn't go to college complained that the schools were turning out people who couldn't even spell or punctuate correctly, much less write interesting letters . . . writing was an unpleasant chore for most students and teachers.

Many of the same complaints are still being voiced today. And while recent approaches to the teaching of writing appear more advanced, they must still be integrated as part of a philosophy that recognizes that new rhetoric is conceived as thought unfolding in the search of truth, however tentative. While traditional rhetoric was concerned with skill in expressing preconceived arguments and points of view, the new rhetoric is concerned with the exploration of ideas. While traditional rhetoric was based on established patterns of discourse, the new rhetoric is based on the assumption that organization grows out of the subject being treated. The new rhetoric, in short, is based on the notion that the basic process of composition is discovery, and not recovery. In the process of composing, the writer or speaker discovers what he really wants to say about a topic, and his effectiveness depends an his ability to communicate what he has learned to his audience.

Ideas are the heartbeat of writing. Write down your ideas.

— Donda Rule #63

It is the broader framework that will be most useful in teaching students to write as it eliminates the tendency of some instructors to focus on approaches that deal only partially with the problems involved in acquiring good writing skills. Helpful though they be, the work of new rhetoricians must still be largely supplemented to include the contributions of others who have developed insights into teaching writing. The work of Kellogg Hunt, although helpful in such aspects as increasing the length of sentences, is inadequate for teaching many other important aspects of writing such as those involving creative thinking. Both Gerald Kincaid and Earl Buxton raised interesting and important issues regarding the writing of freshman college students, but in analyzing the current system of the teaching of written composition, the need remains to view each of the existing theories and methods as partial and as most effective as part of the larger and more important whole. What theories and methods to include as part of a systems methodology for teaching writing is a question that arises after an analysis of the current system and a matter to be addressed more fully in step five of the systems approach. Briefly however, the methods selected depend largely on the individual needs of students.

While some students may benefit immensely from exposure to sentence combining exercises, other students may find less use for such an activity. In any instance, the writing instructor will want to include those activities that reflect the belief that the process of composition is discovery and not recovery, and that the process involves many interrelated parts. Instructors may best arrive at the activities they will use after carefully assessing the needs of their students.

In assessing the needs of students, the second phase of analyzing the system, the teacher of written composition might consider: (1) the class discussion on the teaching of writing, (2) the student papers on education, (3) comments of various rhetoricians, and (4) personal experiences. During the class discussion students may reveal many of their own needs noting implicitly or explicitly problems they may have with such aspects as organization, critical thinking, punctuation, paragraphing, developing ideas, spelling, and so on. While a student may or may not state for example that he finds no need to improve his writing except for the purpose of completing a course requirement or that he is seldom motivated to express his ideas through writing, the astute instructor should recognize these aspects as barriers to the students in improving their writing skills. It is essential that such problems be dealt with. Too often, such needs are lightly regarded if not overlooked completely. But an open and honest discussion about problems students have with writing will aid significantly in identifying needs.

In grading the initial papers of the students, the instructor is able to see more clearly the specific needs of individual students. While one student may need help in learning to compose an effective sentence, another already competent in sentence structure may need work in developing a more effective style of writing. The instructor should be mindful that some students may already be effective writers needing exposure to more advanced techniques. These students may become bored if not challenged to meet their maximum potential. Thus, a problem can be created.

In carefully reviewing the papers of students in search for problem areas, the writing instructor will identify some problems more readily than others. Such aspects as spelling, phrasing, paragraphing, and punctuation are usually not difficult to access. But equally as important as mechanical aspects are such factors as motivation, purpose, and critical thinking. In assessing the individual needs of each student, the writing instructor must consider various aspects of writing as well as individual differences and interests of students. While every student may write on the same general topic, that of education for instance, their viewpoints and level of thinking will vary. One student may find the educational system flawless; another may feel that formal education is dictated by corrupt forces of society offering very little to many students interested in personal growth and development. Whether students display positive or negative attitude toward a subject, their individual papers will encompass expression.

Understanding the Written Composition as a System

Repeatedly, the written composition has been defined as a system with many interrelated parts. In helping students to view the essay as a system, and thus to understand that each element is important alone and in relation to the whole, the instructor might ask students to name elements of the written composition: the title, introduction, body, conclusion, sentences, words, paragraphs, transitions, and so on. Writing them on the board, the instructor should include elements overlooked by students such as thesis statements, topic sentences, punctuation, support, motivation, purpose, and rhetorical devices. Then the teacher may involve the students in a discussion of the importance of these elements as autonomous holons and as interdependent parts. Selecting a particular piece of writing, such as "I Have a Dream," by Martin Luther King, Jr., the instructor then leads the class in a discussion of this particular piece of writing as a system. For King's writing, like all writing, is comprised of many interrelated parts, all of which is important in constituting the whole. The instructor may begin by presenting the work in its entirety, reading it with enthusiasm, attempting to create enthusiasm within the students. Afterward, a focus on individual factors will provide students with information needed to achieve effective writing as they "see the parts" in light of the whole. There are many ways to approach King's work in explaining a system. The teacher may want to begin by asking the students what motivated King to write the speech. Answers will vary from student to student, some pointing out the friction created by an unjust system as a motivating factor, while others may speak more specifically of particular experience that may have motivated King. At any rate, this is an excellent opportunity for the instructor to reiterate the importance of motivation and purpose in writing. Too often, writing teachers, so concerned about the end results, overlook important aspects necessary or helpful in achieving the final student product. Other elements of King's writing should be discussed from the title to the final statement. When students can see clearly how effective writing is achieved, they are more likely to have a better understanding of the written composition as a system.

By numbering each paragraph or sentence, extracting each as a single element of the whole essay, distributing them among the class, and asking students to read the sentences in random order, the teacher is able to demonstrate vividly the importance of putting together elements in a particular manner to yield the comprehensive and more important whole. Students who are able to view the written composition as a phenomena constituted by interrelated parts and who are given an opportunity to study these parts as both autonomous wholes and interdependent parts may gain more confidence in their ability to produce good writing. The instructor may ask students questions such as what made King's introduction effective? How does King use rhetorical devices? What is the central idea of the paper and how is it supported? How does King achieve smooth transitions and why is this necessary in writing a good paper? These are questions that can be raised about all writing, including student writing.

Students who appear to have a basic command of the skill of writing and who seek ways to improve their style may benefit by examining such elements as rhetorical devices. Effective repetition (anaphora) is one of the many rhetorical devices used quite frequently and effectively by King and other writers. Often students are able to use such devices in their own writing to improve the quality of their papers. Again, any rhetorical device is another interrelated, part of the whole, a part that may sometimes make the difference between a boring and interesting essay. There are many ways to approach a study of the many parts of an essay. But by understanding the written composition as a system, no one part need be overlooked as an unimportant element in the development of the whole. Each part can be studied in relative isolation but more importantly as part of the larger structure.

> Use rhetorical devices in your writing. These devices can make your writing more interesting.
>
> — DONDA RULE #64

UNDERSTANDING IMPORTANCE AND POWER OF THE WRITTEN WORD

To give students experiences in understanding and appreciating the importance and power of the written word, the writing instructor might begin by asking students to list ways in which writing of some type is used. Students should be encouraged to include such uses as labels in clothing or on other products, billboards, road signs, medical prescriptions, and legal documents. By pointing out such uses in addition to more common ones such as magazines and books, copy for advertisement and others, the teacher may be able to lead students toward a greater appreciation for writing. Then, both teachers and students should look more closely at what is being said through the use of writing, examining the effect of writing on the world at large. Words have always been used to impress upon the minds of men and women the thoughts and convictions of the writers. In many cases, such words have been as powerful as any medium of expression. Consider the words of Frederick Douglass for example:

> If there is no struggle, there is no progress. Those who profess to favor freedom, yet deprecate agitation are men who want crops without plowing up the ground. They want the rain without thunder and lightning. They want the ocean without the awful roar of its many waters. Power concedes nothing without demand. It never has and it never will. Man may not get all he pays for in this life, but he must certainly pay for all he gets.

This passage by Douglass illustrates that the written word can be a powerful tool. Students might be asked their opinion of this passage and encouraged to notice the vivid images used by the writer to impress upon the minds of the reader. These words, straight forward and uncomplicated, have been quoted by many from the time they were written to the present day. Writing teachers might ask students what effect these words had on Douglass' contemporaries and if they are still relevant and effective today. Students might become more appreciative of writing as a means of effecting change, and thus they may become more interested, perhaps eager to improve their writing skills.

Make your language colorful — or someone may never read your message.

— DONDA RULE #65

In order to facilitate critical thinking on the part of students, there are many strategies the writing teacher may use. The resources that will aid students in forming intelligent opinions and in supporting them are unlimited. They may range from the smallest newspaper article to an adolescent novel; from the lyrics of a popular song to an interesting and provocative television show. Often the writing instructor may encourage critical thinking by presenting a hypothetical problem and asking students to respond by giving and supporting their thoughts and feelings about the problem.

> Use pop culture and hypothetical situations to engage students.
>
> — DONDA RULE #66

The creative teacher will have little if any problems with finding materials to stimulate students in ways that will challenge them to think. One source in particular however, that may be a good starting point for encouraging this crucial aspect of critical thinking is William Golding's "Thinking as a Hobby." This short but thought-provoking essay deals directly with the problem of thinking (or of not thinking). Golding suggests that there are three levels of thought and gives examples of each. Golding defines *grade-three* thought, as feeling rather than thought, noting *grade-three* thinking as hypocrisy, and thoughtless conformity. *Grade-two* thinkers, says Golding, recognize contradictions in a given situation, but have no truthful or viable solutions. They often ask the question, "What is truth?" but they seldom answer it. They destroy without the power to create. On the other hand, the *grade-one* thinker asks the question, "What is truth?" and attempts to answer the question. To Golding, the *grade-one* thinker has a moral, coherent system for living. Just as he is concerned about his family and himself, he is concerned about his fellow man. He lives by the dictates of his own conscience and consciousness rather than by standards that society may try to impose upon him.

In reading "Thinking as a Hobby" students are challenged to think critically and to commit themselves to a search for truth. The new rhetoric is concerned with the unfolding of truth no matter how tentative or aggressive. To write effective papers, students must learn to form opinions and convictions based on their own thinking and their own probing for truth.

Organizing an essay can be approached in a number of ways. Two approaches frequently used include the scratch outline and the write-in. Both of these activities have been used successfully in teaching writing. After a writer has established a definite purpose for writing and has decided on a general topic, they may benefit by jotting down everything that comes to mind about the subject. Suppose the topic is "Why Students Go to College." The instructor might guide the class in a group activity where the students list as many reasons as possible why students go to college. In addition to such common reasons as getting an education, others should be included such as finding a husband or wife, pledging a sorority, singing in the choir, playing sports, peer pressure, parental pressure, Veterans Administration benefits, and so on. After a list of 30 reasons has been completed, the next step is to eliminate repetition. To get an education and to acquire knowledge might both be included on the first list of reasons. Yet one should be eliminated. Reasons should then be grouped into categories —social benefits, financial reasons, and so on. Thus, scholarships, grants, loans, and Veterans Administration benefits would come under the general heading of finance. After students have categorized reasons, they should determine which aspects will be included in the final paper and decide on a general thesis. Although they may not choose to follow the outline precisely (many are limited by such a rigid format), such an organizing element will help them to define more clearly what there is to be said about a subject and how one might go about saying it.

The write-in entails the students' writing on a given subject without regard for anything more than just getting ideas on paper. The object is to keep the pen moving—to express ideas freely without worrying about form or specific development. Revision comes later after basic ideas have been expressed in a rather crude form. Once the writer gets his ideas on paper, no matter how crude they may be, he is able to see clearly, organize, and develop them further. After the initial write-in, much care is taken in developing a well-written paper by adding, deleting, and developing.

Do not edit while writing. Editing can deter and detour great ideas.

— DONDA RULE #67

Developing Interesting and Imaginative Sentences

Just as there are many ways to add color to a picture, there are many ways to add color and detail to the written composition. Whether a writer chooses to narrate, describe, explain, or argue, to be effective they must write clear and interesting sentences. Activities that challenge students to be imaginative and critical thinkers will aid them in producing colorful and well-developed essays. The instructor should stress the importance of detail in writing interesting prose and should assign activities that will help students develop their abilities in this area. One such activity suggested by Christensen requires that students modify as specifically as possible one particular word. For example, they may start with the word "dog" and end up with a sentence such as this: The small spirited brown dog with the spotted tail followed his master to school each day and waited anxiously for the bell to sound, signaling the end of the school day. Suddenly, one word is expanded to over 30 words as more information about the dog gives the reader a clearer and more detailed picture. Students must be encouraged to push for details leaving out nothing that would serve to support a point more fully or describe an event or place more accurately. The teacher begins by asking a student to modify the word *dog*, and thus:

Teacher: dog

Student I: Brown dog
Student II: Brown spirited dog
Student III: Brown spirited dog with spotted tail
Teacher: What did he do?
Student: Followed his master and so on
Teacher: Where to?
Student: School
Teacher: How often?
Student: Each day
Teacher: And what did the dog do at school?
Student: Waited
Teacher: Waited how?
Student: Anxiously

The aim here is to facilitate the writing of colorful and fully detailed sentences. With the application of the appropriate activity whether the one suggested here, or several others, skimpy sentences may become remarkably detailed, and vague ideas, remarkably clear.

In this final step of the systems approach, systems synthesis, and evaluation, a few ways have been suggested to meet specified goals and objectives. But never should a writing instructor view such a list of options as exhaustive. An instructor may find a need to focus attention on T-unit development for example, and would thus need to select activities accordingly. The systems approach, because it is so encompassing, enables the instructor to utilize any activity that will be useful to the students. Also, the options chosen should be evaluated constantly and should be included only so long as they prove effective in helping students to improve their writing skills.

Learning to write well and teaching the art of writing are not simple tasks. They require will power, practice, and patience on the part of both teachers and students. Moreover, they require a broad perspective that allows for the many possibilities in the process of composing. Teachers of writing can ill afford to approach their task from a limited and thus limiting perspective. They must view the writing process from the broadest perspective, one that takes into account that many interrelated and interdependent parts function in particular ways to produce the whole. They must not focus blindly on one aspect of writing without regard for the others. They must understand the interrelatedness among all the parts involved in the process of learning to write effectively and they must share this understanding with students.

> Writing requires will power, practice, and patience.
>
> — Donda Rule #68

Likewise, the student must come to see that writing is achieved through the careful ordering of many related parts. These parts, all of which are important, yield the whole, the essay, the short story, the play, the novel. The parts themselves are not new, and many of the methods used in teaching writing are also old. What is missing is a conceptual framework, a shared perspective regarding the nature of writing so that teachers can present in an integrated manner of what is already known and what we are likely to find out about the writing process. The systems approach is urgently needed because it allows one to view writing from the broadest perspective. Through the use of a systems approach, both teachers and students of writing are likely to experience greater success.

It has not been my aim to develop flowcharts and graphs that typify many so-called systems approaches. It has not been my aim to provide a stockpile of new activities teachers may use in the classroom. It has not been my aim to make mechanical the teaching of writing by insisting on the use of rigid objectives to be followed by all teachers and students. Rather, my purpose has been to suggest, to insist even that those who teach writing and those whose desire it is to improve their writing, need consciously embrace an underlying philosophy that if applied in the classroom, may help to produce astonishing results.

> Practicing composition can produce astonishing results.
>
> — Donda Rule #69

The teacher who has considered the importance of accurately identifying the problem is to be commended. The teacher who has evaluated various options should be praised as well. The teacher who has analyzed the system, and who in doing so, is more knowledgeable and will be better off because of it.

It is apparent, however, that something is still lacking in the teaching of writing. This lacking element is the attitude, the belief, the strong conviction that just as the many views in science finally gave way to a more encompassing view, that of systems theory, the many philosophies in the teaching of written composition must allow for one that is more encompassing, one that acknowledges not only the interrelatedness of the written composition, but of the entire world.

When writing, include a world view — express a single point.

— DONDA RULE #70

The most fundamental purpose of this work has been to suggest that in addition to a conceptual theory of rhetoric itself, or a way to view the process of teaching written composition, teachers and students of writing need an underlying world view that can be internalized and acknowledged as the basis for all writing activities. A systems view of the world and thus of the composing process may result in significant changes in the teaching of writing as well as in the writing ability of students. Just as a physicist should not proceed with an experiment relying on outdated assumptions held in physics, no writing instructor would teach students relying on outdated assumptions.

Writing instructors must undergo a paradigm shift relative not only to the teaching of writing but to the world in general. A systems view is comprehensive in education, specifically in the teaching of writing. It tolerates no approach that fails to produce growth in students' writing. Teachers of written composition, who embrace a systems view, may make better use of existing theories and strategies and create new ones using them all as part of a broader framework in their teaching.

It is not another strategy or another approach that is needed by teachers and students of writing, but a more comprehensive way of looking at the world and the process of composing. Until we are able to view the writing process from the broadest perspective, a systems perspective, we are likely to continue to have relatively little effect on the writing ability of our students.

8
A COMMUNITY-BASED ECONOMIC DEVELOPMENT CURRICULUM FOR FRESHMEN IN CHICAGO PUBLIC SCHOOLS

Dr. Donda West was the lead writer and curriculum specialist for an eco-dev plan for students. The program's efforts were to teach Chicago Public School (CPS) students community improvement through planning and management, health and safety, and technological implementation. She had support from the writing team of Flower, Orr, and Westinghouse, the Bethel New Life Youth Enterprise Network, Nancy J. Barrett, Gloria T. Brown, Tamakisha S. Burden, Elizabeth Ester, Cynthia Felton, Carol Grant Hall, Herman Jackson, Bennie W. Johnson, Althea T. Jones-Ellis, Gloria Lewis, and Tiffany Lewis.

THE PURPOSE OF EDUCATION IS TO PROVIDE STUDENTS WITH THE opportunities and training necessary for vocational and life-long fulfillment. In the community-based economic development (CBED) curriculum that follows, students will learn how to learn and equally as important, they will discover what is important to them and how to sustain healthy, prosperous communities. The underlying premise of this curriculum is that through active participation in meaningful, hands on learning experiences, all students can and will learn. The school is an anchor of the community which needs the input of students, parents, school staff, businesses, and community representatives to develop an effective curriculum and sustain an engaging program. The lessons are designed to encourage students to lead, follow, and become intimately involved with the actual development of some aspect of community. Student ownership and student empowerment are critical elements of implementation as are the concepts of teacher as coach and students as workers.

Eligibility for the Program

All CPS freshmen are eligible. The goal is for students to have opportunities to learn about and demonstrate their understanding of economic development concepts and to apply their knowledge in actual community-based projects that could lead to economic development.

Community Resources as Learning Tools

Using resources such as community development organizations, libraries, churches, government offices, parks and recreation personnel, students will come to understand that education extends far beyond the school walls into the communities where they reside. Students will learn the responsibility and the rewards of entrepreneurship through cooperative learning activities. They will come to value their own abilities as well as the expertise of their coaches (teachers), parents, and community volunteers. Students are also expected to think more broadly of themselves as not just consumers, but eventually as producers of neighborhood goods and services. Students will develop entrepreneurial skills to enhance their personal economic livelihood and neighborhood enhancement.

Instructional/Assessment Strategies & Extended Periods

Facilitators of this curriculum must value the varied learning styles of students, structuring their teaching accordingly. Such awareness and sensitivity to individual students will increase the probability of success for every student in the program. Since the curriculum incorporates non-traditional learning activities, an effective program is best implemented in extended periods. It is therefore suggested that the time allotted for the classes be no less than 80 minutes. Non-traditional assessment strategies that require students to demonstrate genuine understanding of the concepts presented is critical for authentic student achievement. Demonstration of knowledge, skill, and attitudes that will contribute to career and personal success should characterize the major assessment strategies.

Teaching All Aspects of the Industry

It is also critical that the curriculum addresses industry standards including workplace readiness and a working knowledge of all aspects of the industry: planning, management, finance, technical and production skills, underlying principles of technology, labor issues, community issues, and health, safety, and environmental issues. While the specific goals of each class may vary to some extent, the overall goals expected of students upon graduation are challenging and will provide students with a strong sense of accomplishment.

Freshmen CBED classes will provide opportunities that will enable students to begin mastering the overall goals. Specific goals, to be determined jointly by teachers, students, and parents, can be mastered by the close of the semester.

Recognition of Industry Standards

Each school's business advisory team should work with community and school personnel to identify the skills needed in industry. With increased joblessness and neighborhood deterioration so prevalent in many urban communities, a curriculum which focuses on re-building local economies through informed and strategic planning is not only timely, but critical to present and future community development and to the career and personal success of each student.

Students enrolled in the CBED classes will pursue the following general goals and characteristics throughout their high school career:

- High self-esteem/individuality
- Excellent communication skills
- Strong command of basic skills
- Knowledge and practice of, respect and concern for African American culture, other American culture, and cultures worldwide
- Ability to think critically, solve problems, and make wise decisions
- Computer literacy
- Job readiness/workplace skills, ability to work in groups, work ethics
- Competence in community development strategies
- Ability to follow through on tasks until completion
- Economic literacy
- Mastery of vocational skills
- Good attendance (expectations, quality, promptness)
- Civic responsibilities, patriotism, loyalty to country
- Responsibility for own actions
- Valuing of life-long learning and the pursuit of excellence
- Excellence in coursework
- Community involvement
- 7 principles of Nguzo Saba: unity, self determination, collective work and responsibility, cooperative economics, purpose, creativity, faith
- Business ownership skills

SPECIFIC GOALS OF CBED CLASSES

Through CBED and other classes taken in grades 9-12, students can achieve the goals listed above. Specific goals for the CBED classes, however, will be significantly fewer and therefore reachable within the time frame of one semester. Listed are two sets of goals/student outcomes appropriate for CBED classes. Teachers may select either set of goals, select goals from both sets, or develop other goals similar to those listed.

STUDENT OUTCOMES FOR CBED CLASSES—SET I

- Identify community strengths and weaknesses
- Outline necessary steps to rebuild businesses
- Demonstrate life survival skills through authentic performances
- Demonstrate confidence in using learned skills to obtain jobs or careers

Student Outcomes for CBED Classes—Set II

- Understand key terms related to community development and all aspects of the industry
- Articulate health, safety, and environmental issues impacting the community
- Analyze and interpret financial data related to community economic development
- Compare and contrast statistical data of economic development in selected communities

It is immediately apparent that the outcomes in Set I are more general than those listed in Set II. Should an instructor select the Set I outcomes, he or she would, of course, specify particulars. For example, the outcome which reads "demonstrate life survival skills through authentic performances" must be made clearer by the instructor (with student input if possible) so that the student knows precisely what life survival skills must be demonstrated and what performance tasks are acceptable as methods of demonstration. An instructor may include as life survival skills workplace readiness competencies such as dependability, promptness, personal hygiene, appropriate dress, good communication skills, teamwork, and problem solving. If this is done, that instructor must create learning activities that would enable students to develop those skills or characteristics, and design assessment tools (authentic tasks) through which students could demonstrate mastery of those life survival skills.

FLEXIBILITY TO "EVOLVE" THE CURRICULUM

A third option for CBED instructors is to develop their own set of student outcomes based on the concepts to be learned in the course. (See the following section of this guide for concepts.) It is not mandatory that outcomes for the CBED courses be universal across schools, but it is strongly advised that they be universal within schools. Again, specific outcomes may vary to some extent from school to school as long as instructors address all aspects of the industry and specific measurable ways students will actually become involved in CBED. Whether instructors select outcomes in Set I, Set II, or develop their own outcomes to be used uniformly within one given school, outcomes should be:

- Significant
- Attainable
- Measurable
- Meaningful to students
- Well stated, and
- Practical.

SIGNIFICANT OUTCOMES

Determining the significance of an outcome is to some degree subjective. Instructors may raise the legitimate question "significant to whom?" However, a basis for determining significance of an outcome may involve 1) its usefulness beyond the classroom, b) its value in personal student development, and c) its relevance to CBED. For an outcome to be significant, it should be aimed toward some real-world goal that will benefit both student and community.

Attainable Outcomes

In the time frame of one semester, the number of goals to be mastered will be somewhat limited. Nevertheless, teachers should select or develop challenging outcomes. The key consideration should be whether or not all students can be expected to achieve the outcome given students' ability levels and the time constraints imposed.

Measurable Outcomes

Whether an outcome is from the affective or cognitive domain, it should be measurable. That is, the instructor or student (in the case of peer or self assessment) must be able to indicate the degree to which a student has been successful in attaining a particular goal. For concrete outcomes, such as "students will define 20 terms related to community development," the scale of measurement is clear cut. For abstract goals such as those involving self esteem, for example, instructors must research or develop assessment instruments that will measure a student's progress in an area that is more difficult to quantify.

Well-Stated Outcomes Are Meaningful to Students

Regardless of the importance of an outcome to an instructor, unless the students come to appreciate the outcome and respect its purpose, it is unlikely that genuine growth will occur even if the student manages to achieve the outcome. It is well worth the time to explore outcomes together and to confirm students' full understanding and adequate appreciation of outcomes. Only then can instructors expect students to invest wholly in mastery of the outcome. Clarity is critical as an ambiguous outcome is confusing and ultimately detrimental to student progress. Outcomes should be worded so that parallelism, conciseness, and preciseness are apparent. Both students and teachers will be clear on what is expected only when outcomes are effectively stated. An example of a clearly stated outcome: Students will be able to define "urban renewal" accurately and fully discuss its impact on a particular community.

PRACTICAL OUTCOMES

The CBED curriculum is hands-on and its purpose is to inspire real-life community experiences. Students should learn primarily through doing. Involvement in practical activities to achieve practical goals is a necessity.

COURSE CONTENT (CONCEPTS) AND CRITERIA FOR SELECTION

The number of concepts and ideas to be addressed in the CBED classes exceeds the time allowed (20 weeks) for mastery of all of them. Similar to suggestions for selecting specific student outcomes, concept and idea selection can be determined by instructors from school to school with input from a curriculum team including teachers, students, parents, school staff, and especially community representatives with CBED expertise. Instructors are encouraged to select concepts and ideas from the following list from a variety of activities.

LEARNING ACTIVITIES

The opportunities instructors provide for authentic student learning may be the single most important factor in the success of CBED classes. Many instructors, the most caring, dedicated, and talented in fact, must remain aware of the importance of active student involvement on a daily basis. The adage, 'Tell me and I forget, show me and I remember, involve me and I understand" is an appropriate motto for those involved in CBED classes. While knowledge base is important and theory necessary for the basis of practical activity, students learn best in a "doing" environment. It will not be adequate to merely discuss a concept such as proactive intervention, students must proactively intervene. The following list of activities are designed to maximize student involvement and therefore foster genuine and life-long learning.

SUGGESTED LEARNING ACTIVITIES FOR CBED STUDENTS

- Attend park district board meetings
- Research the operating budgets of conservatories and parks
- Research sources of funding for each and explain how funding is allocated
- Teach other students (peer teaching) to reinforce understanding of CBED concepts
- Work in teams on a specific project to develop the community economically
- Volunteer with a community development project to do research that will ultimately contribute to social or economic development
- Keep a journal to chronicle community situations impeding economic development
- Develop partnerships to create revenue to be circulated within the community,
- Create a community development portfolio which includes a neighborhood assets map, list of vacant property, and data on land values
- Create charts and graphs on census data and other community statistics,
- Draw maps of a selected urban community and indicate where economic development is most needed
- Determine what businesses and services are needed in a particular community,
- Physically examine a given community for uncontrolled garbage
- Potholes

- Rodent control
- Absentee landlords
- Gangs
- Drugs
- Animal control
- Child neglect and abuse
- Homelessness
- Suggested learning activities for CBED students
- Abandoned buildings
- Truancy

The particulars of each activity can be developed by teachers, students, community experts or all three. Together the learning team can decide on communities for study. The learning team should also be clear on methods of and time frame for assessment and evaluation at the time the assignment or learning activity is initiated. Cooperative learning is strongly recommended.

Assessment and Evaluation Strategies

Below are some methods of assessing and evaluating students 1) early on in the course (informative assessment), 2) during the course—weeks six through sixteen perhaps (interim assessment), and at or toward the end of the course (summative assessment). Instructors are encouraged to use their own discretion in the use and timing of the assessment and evaluation methods listed and to add creatively to the list.

Formative Assessment

- Role play
- Scenario writing
- On-site community participation
- Class discussion

- Dramatization
- Teacher observation
- Scale drawings
- Journalistic writing
- Performances and demonstrations
- Written and oral reports
- Peer evaluation
- Self-evaluation
- Student constructed exams
- Debates

Summative Assessment (Evaluation)

- Extended projects
- Broadcast presentations
- Videos of performance
- Competitions
- Written and oral exams
- Portfolios

Instructors should remember that assessment sends a message to students. It indicates what is important and what is not. Therefore as much planning and consideration should be put into assessment (and evaluation) as is put into designing learning activities. For assessment is a part of any well-thought out learning activity.

Measurement is a key aspect of evaluation, but creative measurement scales are frequently necessary in the non-traditional curriculum. Attitude toward work cannot necessarily be measured using traditional methods and instructors must create evaluation scales that will indicate a student's attitude toward work. Assessment should be as useful to the instructor as it is to the student.

Project

Develop a real estate investment firm designed to 1) help rid your community of abandoned buildings, 2) provide housing for the homeless, and 3) generate income for your community (as this is a community-owned business). Write a full-scale plan of how this venture will be approached from start to finish. In your business description—which should reflect short and long-term goals—discuss what is necessary in terms of each aspect of the industry. What planning, management, finance, technical and production skills, underlying principles of technology, labor issues, community issues, and health, safety, and environmental issues would or might be critical in the success of this community-based venture?

With the directives as a starting point, instructors may proceed by assigning teams of 2-4 students to examine, explore, and define one particular aspect of the industry. It will be the responsibility of respective teams to demonstrate a thorough understanding of the aspect assigned to them as well as an understanding of how it works in actuality. Each team will have the further responsibility of explaining its aspect of the industry to the other members of the class and determining that all members of the class fully understand the aspect. Then two representatives from each team will form a nucleus group to articulate how planning and all other aspects will be implemented in the real estate investment venture. Students will actually plan, research, and become otherwise involved as though they will actually purchase real-estate. But the actual purchasing may be on paper only (with realistic finance plans) unless teachers and schools have outlets for making actual purchases.

Upon completion of the real-life and hypothetical activities, each student should be able to demonstrate adequate understanding of the role each aspect plays in such a venture.

On a small scale, teachers may develop entrepreneurial projects that the class can actually see through to the end. For example, students might develop and actually launch a small manufacturing company housed in the school. The product manufactured should be something students would purchase such as greeting cards, personalized t-shirts, flowers, stylized and customized gifts for special occasions.

Students would manufacture and sell the items and must research fully the application of each aspect of the industry to the business venture launched. Each aspect of the industry could be a department of the company and students would be required to continue effective inclusion of the aspect and make bi-monthly reports on department activities.

CBED instructors are encouraged to be creative and to develop ideas for incorporating all aspects of the industry into the CBED class. Considerable teacher direction may be needed initially so that students find the resources to explore practical application of all aspects of the industry as presented in the Carl D. Perkins Vocational and Technical Act.

STUDENT LEADERSHIP DEVELOPMENT

Instructors must take particular care to facilitate student leadership skills by involving students in activities that will increase their capacity to take initiative, exercise choice, and work collaboratively.

Such activities will involve a concerted effort to promote critical thinking and to encourage students to make sound decisions on their own. Direction from the instructor is critical. But even more critical is that students eventually identify community problems or opportunities themselves, create ways to address them, and exercise initiative and follow-through necessary for effective solutions.

PARENT DEVELOPMENT

Successful school programs frequently are those where parental involvement is considerable. Instructors or other school personnel must actively solicit parental involvement and structure the program so that parents will find their input important and useful. It is imperative that parents are actively engaged in activities that will contribute to program success. This means careful, collaborative planning among a team which is inclusive of parents. It is also extremely beneficial for parents to discuss among themselves ways in which they can contribute to the development of their children via the community-based economic development classes. Some suggested activities include:

- Accompanying students on neighborhood walks and other off-campus learning experiences,
- Assisting students with neighborhood data collection,
- Helping to establish school-based entrepreneurial ventures
- Contacting community and business representatives for class presentations, and
- Assisting students with the manufacturing or production of goods to be sold in school-based businesses.

COMMUNITY-BASED ECONOMIC DEVELOPMENT COURSE OUTLINE

- Identify strengths and weaknesses of selected communities
- Understand key terms related to community development
- Articulate a working definition of the eight aspects of industry
- Outline necessary steps to rebuild businesses in the community
- Compare and contract statistical data of economic development in two specified communities
- Design a community development project that could be implemented in their community work in teams of four to develop a glossary of terms related to urban renewal. At the end of the week, through an academic decathlon, students will demonstrate their understanding of all urban renewal terms.

9
RUSSIAN CULTURE AND LITERATURE IMPLEMENTATION PLAN

A RUSSIAN CULTURE and Literature Implementation Plan was submitted by Dr. Donda C. West at Chicago State University. West had a strong affinity for the Golden Age of Russian Poetry. She enjoyed the works of Alexander Pushkin, Mikhail Lermontov, Fyodor Tyutchev, Evgeny Baratynsky, and novelist, Vladimir Nabokov. The information gained regarding the multi-faceted and intriguing country of Russia and its writers was shared with Chicago State University students in January of 1999. This was also the year Kanye started to work on his definitive debut studio album, The College Dropout.

DONDA WEST EXAMINES BLACK WRITERS IN UNCOMMON PLACES

Donda West taught English 267, a bridge course that fostered a hybrid of Black American Literature and Russian Negro Literary figures. The Spring 1999 course was entitled *An Introduction to Russian Culture and Literature*. The course content included materials and information attained at the University of Iowa, the country of Russia, and through independent study. Students were exposed to various aspects of Russian culture (e.g., politics, economics, education, poetry), African literature, Pushkin as a descendant of Abram Petrovich Gannibal, selected Russian authors and their works, with an emphasis on the quintessential writer, Alexander Pushkin.

West anticipated that the course would generate considerable interest in Russian culture, as the course was taught from an African-centered perspective. Attached is the syllabus for the Spring 1999 semester.

COURSE SYLLABUS

English 267: Introduction to Russian Culture and Literature
Dr. Donda West, Professor
Required Reading:
From Nyet to Da: Understanding the New Russia - Yale Richmond
Russia First: Breaking with the West - Peter Truscott
Russia and the Negro - Allison Blakely
Alexander Pushkin: Complete Prose Fiction - Paul Debreczeny

PURPOSE

The purpose of this course is to expose students to the culture and literature of Russia and the contributions of Russians who were of African descent. Russian politics, economics, and educational structures will be explored and this exploration will serve as a backdrop to the study of Black Russians. Since the early eighteenth century, the world's academics knew that there were [Blacks] in Russia. Later in the last two centuries came word from Russia's Caucasus Mountains of a 'Negro' settlement on the northeastern shores of the Black Sea. Increasingly, 'Negroes' came to Tsarist Russia as free persons of their own choice. Students in this course will examine Russia as it exists today and historically, focusing in general on the country at large, and in particular, on the Black presence in Russia.

. . .

Course Requirements

All students are expected to attend class regularly and submit assignments on time. Late work will not be accepted for any reason and make-up work will be assigned at the discretion of the instructor. The university attendance policy will be strictly adhered to and the instructor reserves the right to drop students from the course should they miss six class sessions.

A mid-term and final exam will be administered as well as several announced exams through the term. Final grades will be based on written assignments (30%), course exams (30%), a final paper (30%), and class participation (10%). Individual conferences with the instructor are invited and encouraged.

Concepts and Coverage for Semester

- An Overview of Russian History and Culture—From Peter the Great to the Present.
- Russian Relations with the West—Foreign Policy Then and Now, Gorbachev and Yeltsin
- Russia's Economy, the Military—Industrial Complex and the Mafia
- The Impact of the 1995 Duma Elections on Russia's Political Landscape Midterm exam
- Writing Assignment #1
- Russia Revisited: The Black Presence—An Overview
- Imperial Russia
- "Negroes" of the Black Sea Region
- Black Servants in Imperial Russia
- Russia and Black Africa
- Writing Assignment #2
- Black Immigrants and Visitors and the Russian Response
- The "Negro" in Russian Art
- Exam #1
- Soviet RussiaBlack Sea "Negroes" in Soviet Society

- The Black "Pilgrims"
- Writing Assignment #3
- The Soviet Perception of the American "Negro Question"
- The USSR and Black Africa
- The "Negro" in Soviet Art
- Blacks in Russia Today—"Baby-Boomer" Re-defined
- Alexander Pushkin—His Life and Selected Works
- Final Exam and Final Paper

BIBLIOGRAPHY

ACKOFF, Russell. L. *Redesigning the Future: A Systems Approach to Social Problems*. New York: Wiley Press, 194.

Alley, Alvin. D. "Creative Thinking and Rhetoric: Implications of Selected Theories of Creativity for the Teaching of Rhetoric in the Secondary Schools." Ph.D. dissertation, Florida State University, 1967.

Bertalanffy, Ludwig Von. *General Systems Theory*. New York: George Braziller, Inc. 1968.

Bockart, John P. A Method for the Integrated Use of Learning Resources in Education." Journal of Higher Education 44 (April 1973):281- 288.

Booth, Wayne. *Modern Dogma and the Rhetoric of Assent*. Indianapolis: University of Notre Dame Press, 1974.

Braddock, Richard; Lloyd-Jones, Richard; and Schoer, Lowell. *Research in Written Composition*. Champaign: National Council of Teachers of English, 193.

Brooks, Linda Yvonne. "The Effect of a Study of Generative Rhetoric on the Syntactic Fluency of Seventh Graders." Ph.D. dissertation, Auburn University, 1975.

Bruner, Jerome S. "On Voluntary Action and Its Hierarchical Structures." In *Beyond Reductionism: New Perspectives in the Life Sciences*, pp. 60-171. Edited by Arthur Koestler and J.R. Smythies. New York: The Macmillan Co., 1969.

Burke, Virginia. *The Paragraph in Context*. Indianapolis: Bobbs-Merrill, 1969.

Buxton. Earl W. "An Experiment to Test the Effects of Writing Frequency and Guided Practice Upon Students' Skill in Written Expression." Ph.D. dissertation, Stanford University, 1958. A synopsis published in *Alberta Journal of Educational Research* 5 (June 1959):91-99.

Carter, Launor F. "The Systems Approach to Education: Mystique and Reality." *The Educational Technology Review Series: Introduction to the Systems Approach* (1973).

Christensen, Francis. *A New Rhetoric*. New York: Harper & Row, 1976.

Combs, Warren E. "Further Effects of Sentence-Combining Practice on Writing Ability." Ph.D. dissertation, University of Michigan, 1976. A synopsis published in *Research in the Teaching of English* 10 (September 1976):72-83.

Cooper, Charles R.; and Odell, Lee; eds. *Research on Composing: Points of Departure*. Urbana, Illinois: National Council of Teachers of English, 1978.

Corbett, Edward P. J. Classical Rhetoric for the Modern Student. New York: Oxford University Press, 1971.

D'Angelo, Frank. *A Conceptual Theory of Rhetoric*. Cambridge: Winthrop Publishers, Inc., 1975.

Dworkin, Martin S., ed. *Dewey on Education*. New York: Teachers College Press, 1959.

Edwards, Clifford H. "Community Involvement in a Systems Approach to Curriculum." *High School Journal* 56 (January 1973):165-171.

Emig, Janet. *The Composing Process of Twelfth-Graders. Research Report No. 13*. Champaign: National Council of Teachers of English, 1971.

Flannigan, John C. "Project PLAN." *Clearing House* 43 (September 1968): 6l-60.

Erikson, Bo. "A Systems Approach to Educational Technology." *Educational Technology* 9 (June 1969):59-70.

Evans, William H.; and Walker, Jerry L. *New Trends in Teaching English in Secondary Schools*. Chicago: Rand McNally & Company, 1966.

Feigenbaum, I., Bartley, D. E., and Politzer, R. L. (1973, 09). Practice-Centered Teacher Training: Standard English for Speakers of Nonstandard Dialects. *TESOL Quarterly,* 7(3), 329. doi:10.2307/3585683

Frank, Lawrence, K. "Social Systems and Culture." In *Toward a Unified Theory of Human Behavior*, pp. 187-203. Edited by Roy Grinker. New York: Basic Books, Inc., 1956.

Friere, Paulo. *Pedagogy of the Oppressed*. New York: The Seabury Press, 1974.

Golding, William. "Thinking As A Hobby." In *Staircase to Writing and Reading: A Rhetoric and Anthology*, pp. 300-307. Edited by Alan Casty and Donald Tighe. Englewood Cliffs: Prentice-Hall, Inc., 1974.

Graves, Richard. "A Strategy for Teaching Sentence Sense." In *Rhetoric and Composition: A Sourcebook for Teachers*, pp. 86-94. Edited by Robert W. Boynton. Rochelle Park: Hayden Book Co., 1976.

Grinker. Roy R., ed., *Toward a Unified Theory of Human Behavior*. New York: Basic Books. Inc., 1956.

Guth. Hans P. *English for a New Generation*. New York: McGraw-Hill, 1973.

Harris, Ronald J. "An Experimental Inquiry Into the Functions and Value of Formal Grammar in the Teaching of English to Children Aged Twelve to Fourteen." Ph.D. dissertation. University of London. 1962. A synopsis published in *Research in Written Composition*. pp. 137-149. Edited by Richard Braddock, Richard Lloyd-Jones and Lawall Schoer. Champaign: National Council of Teachers of English, 1963.

Hartley, Harry J. "Limitations of Systems Analysis." *Education Digest* 35 (October 1969):26-31.

Hayman, John L. Jr. "The Systems Approach and Education." *The Educational Forum* 38 (May 1974):491-502.

Hirsch, E. D. *The Philosophy of Composition*. Chicago: The University Press of Chicago, 197.

Hoetker. James; Sichtenau, Robert; and Farr, Hellen L. K. *Systems, Systems Approaches, and the Teacher*. Chicago: National Council of Teachers of English, 1972.

Hunt, Kellogg W. Grammatical Structures Written at Grade Levels. Research Report No.3. Champaign: National Council of Teachers of English, 1965.

Irmscher, Willlam F. *The Nature of Literature*. New York: Holt, Rinehart and Winston, Inc., 1975.

Kaufman, Roger A. "Systems Approaches to Education: Discussion and Attempted Integration." In *Social and Technological Change: Implications for Education*, pp. 78-85. Edited by Robert E. Corrigan. Englewood Cliffs: Prentice-Hall, 1972.

Kincaid, Gerald L. "Some Factors Affecting Variations in the Quality of Student Writings." Ed.D. dissertation, Michigan State University, 1953.

King, Martin Luther, Jr. "I Have A Dream." In *I Have A Dream: The Life and Times of Martin Luther King, Jr.*, pp , 261-264. Edited by Lenwood G. Davis. Hartsfield: Negro Universities, 1969.

Loestler, Arthur. "Beyond Atomism and Holism: The Concept of the Halon." In *Beyond Reductionism: New Perspectives in the Life Sciences*, pp. 189-202. Edited by Arthur Koestler and J. R. Smythies. New York: The Macmillan Co., 1969.

Kuhn, Thomas S. *The Structure of Scientific Revolutions*. Chicago: The University of Chicago Press, 1962.

Labov, W. (n.d.). 1966–2006. *The Social Stratification of English in New York City,* 380–403. doi:10.1017/cbo9780511618208.018

Laszlo, Ervin. *The Systems View of the World*. New York: George Braziller, Inc., 1972.

Lerner, Daniel, ed. *Parts and Wholes*. New York: The Free Press of Glencoe, 1963.

Martin, E. W., Jr. "The Systems Concept." In *Systems, Organizations, Analysis, Management: A Book of Readings*, pp. 47-62. Edited by David Cleland and William King. New York: McGraw-Hill Book Co., 1969.

Matson, Floyd W. *The Broken Image*. New York: Doubleday & Co., 1966.

McElroy, Robert R. "Why Can't Johnny Write? *Newsweek* 56 (December 8, 1975):58-61.

Melmed, P. J. (1973, 04). "Black-White Speech Relations." Walt Wolfram, Nona H. Clarke. *American Anthropologist, 75*(2), 497-498. doi:10.1525/aa.1973.75.2.02a00970

Mellon, John C. *Transformational Sentence Combining. Research Report No. 10*. Champaign: National Council of Teachers or English, 1-69.

Milsum, John H. "The Hierarchical Basis for General Living Systems." In *Trends in General Systems Theory*, pp. 144-153. Edited by George Klir. New York: John Wiley & Sons, Inc., 1972.

Oettinger, Anthony G. *Run, Computer, Run: The Mythology of Educational Innovation*. Cambridge: Harvard University Press, 1969.

Ofiesh, Gabriel D. "The New Education and the Learning Industry." *Educational Leadership* 26 (May 1969):239-248.

O'Hare, Frank. *Sentence Combining: Grammar Instruction. Research Report No. 1*. National Council of Teachers of English, 1973.

Pierson, Howard. *Teaching Writing*. Englewood Cliffs: Prentice-Hall, Inc., 1972.

Randall, Ronald R. "Perspectives on the Instructional System." *National Technology* (February 1969):6-14.

Ritchie, Barbara. *The Mind and Heart of Frederick Douglass*. New York: Thomas Y. Crowell Company, 1968.

Ryan, T. Antoinette. "Systems Techniques for Programs for Counseling and Counselor Education." *Educational Technology* 38 (May 1974): 46-53.

Sale, Roger. *On Writing*. New York: Random House, 1970.

Shaughnessy, Mina P. *Errors and Expectations: A Guide for the Teacher of Basic Writing*. New York: Oxford university Press, 1977.

Sheils, Merrill. "Why Johnny Can't Write." *Newsweek* 92 (8 December 1975): 58-65.

Silvern, Leonard. "Introduction." *Educational Technology* 9 (June 1969):1-4.

Sledd, James. *English Linguistics: An Introductory Reader*. Chicago: Scott Foresman, 1970.

Weiss, Paul A. "The Living System: Determinism Stratified." In *Beyond Reductionism: New Perspectives in the Life Sciences*, pp. 4- 9. Edited by Arthur Koestler and J. R. Smythies. New York: The Macmillan Co., 1969.

Whorf, Benjamin Lee. *Language, Thought and Reality*. Cambridge: The MIT Press, 1956.

Wooten, Leland. "The Systems Approach to Education as Viewed from the Classroom." *Education* 91 (February 1971):211-219.

Young, Richard E.; Pike, Kenneth; and Becker, Alton. *Rhetoric: Discovery and Change*. New York: Harcourt, Brace & World, 1970.

ABOUT THE EDITOR

Garrard McClendon is an associate professor of Educational Leadership and Policy Studies at Chicago State University. He is the author of *Ax or Ask? - The African American Guide to Better English* and the editor of the *Ebonics Anthologies*. McClendon's research areas include administrators' perceptions of language and dialect, the influence of education law, and the power of school finance. His publications include studies on Ebonics and how teachers use language bias against Black students.

McClendon earned an Emmy Award for Outstanding Achievement in Interview/Discussion for the *Challenge of Raising Black Boys* on WYCC-PBS. He hosts the *McClendon Minute Podcast* and has hosted the television shows, *Garrard McClendon Live on CLTV*, *CounterPoint* and *Off 63rd* on PBS. McClendon is a recipient of the Associated Press Community Impact Award, NAACP Champion Award, a Human Relations Commission Leadership Award, and the Monarch Award. He is the Executive Director of the Milton & Ruby McClendon Scholarship Fund, and he sits on the boards of the Sheila A. Doyle Foundation, the Mid-America Club of Chicago, Art of Culture Foundation, and the National Association of Wabash Men. He is also the director of the anti-violence film, "Forgiving Cain."

Garrard and his wife live in Chicago.

facebook.com/garrardmcclendon

instagram.com/garrardmcclendon

twitter.com/garrardmc

youtube.com/garrardmc

www.ingramcontent.com/pod-product-compliance
Lightning Source LLC
Chambersburg PA
CBHW020829020526
44118CB00032B/408